T0334036

This is a brave and compelling book. Filmmaker and interdisciplinary scholar Agnieszka Piotrowska introduces the notion of the 'nasty woman' into film scholarship, brilliantly updating discussions of the *femme fatale*, and looking afresh at female subjectivity, power and erotic energy. In writing that is gritty, lively, and sometimes personal, partial and sensitive, Piotrowska engages with debates about #MeToo, and feminist killjoys, as she also looks back to Antigone to think through ways of not giving up on one's desire.

Emma Wilson, Professor of French Literature
and the Visual Arts, University of Cambridge, UK

In this volume, Piotrowska has named a new cinematic archetype. The 'nasty woman', written by a woman, directed by a woman, harks back to Antigone and Medusa, and draws on the *femme fatale*, but is a thoroughly modern model for our times. Drawing on feminist theory and psychoanalysis, this timely intervention in film theory tackles women whom we don't have to like, but about whom we want to know more.

Lucy Bolton, Senior Lecturer in Film Studies,
Queen Mary University of London, UK

This book offers up a timely, incisive analysis of the representation of 'bad' women in contemporary cinema – those whose moral choices and troubling, embodied actions mark an ethical shift in our current contemporary climate. Framed through a direct reference to Donald Trump's referral to his political rival, Hillary Clinton, as a 'nasty woman', Pietrowska carefully re-examines seminal films such as Arnold's *Red Road* and Polley's *The Stories We Tell*, drawing on a range of theoretical contexts from Lacanian theory to Laura Marks.

Davina Quinlivan, Senior Lecturer in Performance
and Screen Studies, Kingston University, UK

In a series of highly thought-provoking film analyses Agnieszka Piotrowska re-writes the *femme fatale* as a 'nasty woman' who is a danger not just to men but also to cinema's notion of woman. The figure of Antigone is central to her account of a feminine agency that does not give up on her desire but which is also not simply a matter of revenge. Instead, Piotrowska shows how each film demonstrates the entanglement of drive and desire, of sex and violence in being a feminine subject. *The Nasty Woman* looks awry at the films it discusses, exposing their paradoxical subversion of both cinema's and feminism's binaries in writing that is highly engaging as both scholarly and personal.

Professor Emeritus Elizabeth Cowie,
Film Studies, University of Kent, UK

The Nasty Woman and
the Neo Femme Fatale
in Contemporary Cinema

The Nasty Woman and the Neo Femme Fatale in Contemporary Cinema puts forward the theoretical notion of the 'nasty woman' as a means of examining female protagonists in contemporary culture and cinema, particularly films directed by women. The phrase is taken from an insult thrown at Hillary Clinton during the 2016 Presidential election debates and reclaimed by the feminists worldwide. The volume also draws from the figure of the *femme fatale* in film noir.

Piotrowska presents 'the nasty woman' across cultural and mythical landscape as a figure fighting against the entitlement of the patriarchy. The writer argues that in films such as *Zero Dark Thirty*, *Red Road*, *Stories We Tell*, and even *Gone Girl* the 'nastiness' of female characters creates a new space for reflection on contemporary society and its struggles against patriarchal systems. The nasty woman or neo *femme fatale* is a figure who disrupts stable situations and norms; she is pro-active and self-determining, and at times unafraid to use dubious means to achieve her goals. She is often single, but when married she subverts and undermines the fundamental principles of this patriarchal institution.

For students and researchers in Cultural Studies, Women's, Gender and Sexuality Studies, Film Studies and Psychoanalysis in Film Studies, *The Nasty Woman and the Neo Femme Fatale in Contemporary Cinema* offers an original way of thinking about female creativity and subjectivity. It is also a proud celebration of feminist and female authorship in contemporary Hollywood.

Agnieszka Piotrowska is a filmmaker and a theorist. She is best known for her award-winning cult documentary *Married to the Eiffel Tower*, screened globally in 60 countries. She has written extensively on psychoanalysis, gender and post-colonial culture, setting up creative collaborations in Zimbabwe. She is the author of *Psychoanalysis and Ethics in Documentary Film* (2014) and *Black and White: Cinema, politics and the arts in Zimbabwe* (2017). She is a Reader in Film Practice and Theory at the University of Bedfordshire, UK, and a Visiting Professor at the University of Gdansk, Poland.

The Nasty Woman and the Neo Femme Fatale in Contemporary Cinema

Agnieszka Piotrowska

Routledge
Taylor & Francis Group

LONDON AND NEW YORK

First published 2019
by Routledge

2 Park Square, Milton Park, Abingdon, Oxfordshire OX14 4RN
52 Vanderbilt Avenue, New York, NY 10017

Routledge is an imprint of the Taylor & Francis Group, an informa business

First issued in paperback 2020

British Library Cataloguing-in-Publication Data
A catalogue record for this book is available from the British Library

Library of Congress Cataloging-in-Publication Data
A catalog record for this book has been requested

ISBN: 978-1-138-58644-4 (hbk)
ISBN: 978-0-367-49299-1 (pbk)

Typeset in Times New Roman
by Apex CoVantage, LLC

For Leo and For Helena

Contents

List of figures   x
Instead of a foreword   xi
Acknowledgements   xiii

Introduction: nasty women and neo *femme fatales*   1

1   *Zero Dark Thirty*: 'war autism' or a Lacanian
    ethical act?   25

2   The killjoy and the nasty woman in *Gone Girl* and
    The Girl on the Train   43

3   The nasty woman as a deceiver and a creator in
    Sarah Polley's *Stories We Tell*   65

4   The *non-femme fatale* in *Red Road*   85

    Conclusion: where else will the nasty woman
    go – final nomadic remarks   105

Index   117

Figures

0.1 The 'perfect housewife' (Delphine Seyrig) in *Jeanne Dielman* (Chantal Akerman 1975) — 5

1.1 Maya (Jessica Chastain) in *Zero Dark Thirty*, staring at a blank computer screen waiting for a reply (Kathryn Bigelow 2012) — 35

1.2 Žižek's organisation of ethics and morality into a semiotic square — 36

2.1 Diagram evoking the different ideas and emotions present in this chapter — 43

2.2 Amy Dunne (Rosamund Pike) in the opening scene of *Gone Girl* (David Fincher 2014) — 51

3.1 'Archival fake footage' in *Stories We Tell* (Sarah Polley 2012) — 66

4.1 Sex scene between Clyde (Tony Curran) and Jackie (Kate Dickie) in *Red Road* (Andrea Arnold 2006) — 91

5.1 The mysterious 'fishman' (Doug Jones) and Eliza (Sally Hawkins) in *The Shape of Water* (Guillermo del Toro 2017) — 114

Instead of a Foreword

Now more than ever, it has become important to be clear in establishing the position from which one speaks and not be afraid to do so. To avoid doubt, we need to identify two types of nasty woman. The 'nasty woman' in this book deploys her nastiness in order to fight patriarchy. This 'nasty woman' is not nasty per se; she is nasty because she has to be in order to shift the expected sequence of events in culture and cinema, and therefore in society. The volume discusses films which sow seeds of defiance in the world, the very beginnings of the re-imagining of the familiar tale in which a prince marries a princess and they live happily ever after, with the princess not having a voice or agency of her own. The opposite type of Nasty woman supports Trump, Kavanaugh's Supreme Court nomination, and carries a banner announcing #Himtoo instead of #Metoo. Not the woman in this volume. Her agency might be corrupted by the continuous assault of patriarchy but her heart is – or used to be – in the right place. The woman's rage in the films examined in this volume is metaphorical. It is important to bear in mind that an ability to imagine a situation in which a woman is a subject and not an object, and has agency of her own, is still a radical political gesture in contemporary culture.

Taylor Swift, the highly successful American pop singer with a brand of a 'nice girl', avoided proclaiming her political allegiances until October 2018, when she announced publicly that she would support the Democratic candidates in the forthcoming US elections. Her tweet said 'the old Taylor can't come to the phone right now', echoing her successful music video *Look What You Made Me Do*, in which she adopts the persona of a very nasty woman indeed, a cross between a Goth and a dominatrix, who takes charge and becomes 'harder'. She sings 'in the nick of time' so that she can fight the extreme maleness of our culture.

The announcement regarding her political allegiance encouraged thousands of young voters to register in the US.

Meanwhile, in Britain, a die-hard advocate of maleness, the acclaimed writer Howard Jacobson, in his BBC broadcast of 14th October 2018, confessed how much he objected to the word 'patriarchy' or 'the patriarchy' as he felt it was too academic and did not connect to the real world. He thought the word derisory until the Kavanaugh hearing, in which he witnessed patriarchy at its most entitled and nauseating, observing the united forces mustered in defence of the candidate 'their minds locked, their teeth bared, their eyes as red as the wolves in the night': that was patriarchy embodied. Finally, even Jacobson, this defender of the bastion of maleness in society, conceded that patriarchy needed to be fought against; for if left unchallenged, it would lead to continuous abuses of power. Jacobson finished his talk by stating 'only women can fix us now'.

This book wants to imagine a different future in which patriarchy is indeed the obsolete and absurd word of the past, in which creative imaginings of different 'nomadic' kinds are possible. For now, it focuses on the nasty woman who is herself militant and nasty not because she wants to be but because this sadly still appears the only way by which anything is going to be 'fixed'.

Agnieszka Piotrowska

Acknowledgements

I am very grateful to my institution, the University of Bedfordshire, for allowing me time and space to work in a creative way and in particular my thanks go to my Head of the Department, Jane Carr and the Director of the Research Institute, Alexis Weedon as well as our Dean, Jan Domin. I am grateful for the personal support and faith of Noha Mellor and to my PhD student Priyanka Verma for believing this is a project of relevance across cultures.

I am grateful to my publisher Alexandra McGregor for believing in the timeliness of the book and urging me to focus my energies on writing it quickly. Slavoj Zizek let me re-print his diagram in Chapter 1 and I am delighted to be allowed to use a long quote from Anna Janko's novel *Passion According to St Hanna* in Chapter 4. Parts of Chapter 1 have been previously published in the *New Review of Television and Film Studies*. I am grateful for all the permissions.

Over the years various parts of the volume have been presented at Film Philosophy, BAFTSS (British Association for Television and Screen Studies) and Nordic Summer University events and conferences and I wish to say 'thank you' for the feedback, critique and inspiration to many colleagues and in particular to Will Brown, Kate Ince, Kriss Ravetto Biagolli, Richard Rushton and Ben Tyrer.

I am deeply indebted in every way to Elizabeth Cowie who has been an inspirational presence and a guiding light in my scholarship and life for many years and to Emma Wilson who has taught me to value my film practice as a source of knowledge, and has been unfailingly supportive and encouraging. I am very grateful to Thomas Elsaesser for his enthusiasm for the project, for his generous critiquing of the large chunks of the manuscript and thus for offering a valuable space for intellectual sparring and creative reflection. It would have been a very different volume without our heated arguments.

Last but not least, my huge thanks go to Warren Buckland who has not only supported me as a friend and colleague but has been immensely generous in offering his invaluable practical help in preparing this volume for publication.

Introduction

Nasty women and neo *femme fatales*

The nasty woman and '#MeToo'

On 5th March 2017 the Metropolitan Museum of Art in New York initiated a tour that featured 'the nasty woman' in art across the ages. The museum guide says: 'This is a tour about feisty women who broke the rules. Flaunting convention, they reached for power and influence, and shaped the culture and politics of their day. People call them "nasty women", but they still admire them. And along the way they became the subjects of great works of art – many of them on display at the Met'.[1] In terms of the arts, the tour includes depictions of Medusa, Judith cutting off the head of Holofernes, but also portraits of various courtesans and queens. It is faintly amusing to notice that whilst the tour was advertised as a nasty woman tour the link sent the reader to the websites called 'shady ladies' – perhaps unwittingly presenting unconscious connotations of the organisers (is a nasty woman by definition a shady one?).

The idea of a nasty woman who challenges the masculine might is not new but in recent times it has gained a new currency and offers a new space for reflection: what does it mean to be a nasty woman in the contemporary world and why and how might it be relevant?

This book puts forward the term 'nasty woman' as a possible theoretical concept to use in contemporary cinema alongside or perhaps including the neo *femme fatale*. The 'nasty woman' in this volume draws from the figure of the *femme fatale* in film noir but she is not necessarily a *femme fatale* in the sense of the word used in the 40s and 50s classic cinema – of which more later in this introduction. Whilst strong, confrontational and often somewhat transgressive, she is not an action woman, or a heroine of a horror film.[2] The nasty woman discussed here is the creation of a woman writer, director or producer, and she is recognisably like the rest of us – at least to begin with. She is not a fantastical creature, although I suggest here that her characterisation draws from some classic archetypes.

I borrow the term 'nasty woman' from the famous Trump phrase about Hillary Clinton during the 2016 presidential campaign that evoked a massive solidarity response on the part of women globally (see Gray (2016)). This phrase, which revealed Trump's thinly veiled nonreformed and ultra conservative misogynist persona, was confirmed and re-confirmed by a variety of scandals including his admission of having no scruples over touching women's private parts.[3] It is of course ironic that Hillary Clinton in the end was unable to withstand the ultra patriarchal nasty man that Trump embodies. The reasons no doubt are complex: the email scandal, the general rise of populism, and a whole range of other political and economic issues but also perhaps because of her own association to the patriarchal system, through her husband and *his* various sexual affairs and indiscretions that she was then alleged to have ignored. In her own book she acknowledges that at the beginning of this very televised encounter she felt crowded and bullied by Trump in a physical way – but was unable to call him out because she felt she needed to appear well balanced, strong and – well yes, nice (Clinton 2017: 136). In a way, she was not quite 'nasty' enough in her own right and ended up being perceived as a part of a patriarchal dynasty rather than a pioneer.[4]

In this Introduction I offer two theoretical positions relating to the 'nasty woman' figure. They both come from archetypal mythical characters reformulated by theoretical feminist thinking and offer a productive space to discuss a new *femme fatale* in contemporary English speaking cinema. These figures are Medusa and Antigone – and I will return to them in due course. Whilst the book is about cinema, it is also about our contemporary culture and the woman's position in it. In this Introduction in particular, I will offer a number of cultural tropes with a view of it opening a space for reflection on contemporary sexual and gender identities, perhaps not quite as fluid as some theorists would have us believe.[5]

One could argue that, culturally, the notion of 'the nasty woman' is a very familiar concept. It has many guises and comes in many forms in history, myths, legends and storytelling, not necessarily just those familiar in the Western culture. In most cultures, however, as well as in Western fairytales, the figure of a nasty and powerful woman who is able to undermine the patriarchal systems, at times armed with supernatural powers, is often associated with the loss of her sexual attractiveness as if nobody would bother to argue with men if they could seduce them sexually.[6] In this book, and in particular in Chapter 2, on *Gone Girl* (2014) and *Girl on the Train* (2016), I will be thinking of Sara Ahmed's ideas from her recent book *Living a Feminist Life* (2017: 38). In particular, her idea of the 'feminist killjoy' seems close to the 'nasty woman' notion: a feminist who disrupts stable situations and norms, if necessary at a high cost to herself – and to others. The killjoy and the nasty woman are done with the normative requirement for any woman of being 'nice'. We will see how in practice the killjoy, when she gets going, can kill rather more than 'joy', although that too.

In this short book I will be mostly bracketing the older 'nasty woman' who, in forms of witches and various stepmothers in fairytales, has become an archetype of a powerful nasty woman able to take on the patriarchal system across cultures and societies. I will mention such examples in passing as secondary figures but, for reasons that I will elaborate on, I will be focusing on younger women who have been written by and created for contemporary cinematic texts as characters who have chosen to be 'nasty' even though they still can easily gain patriarchal favours by being more pleasant and amenable. They become that for various reasons, emerging out of various motivational storyworlds which I will discuss further – primarily as a deliberate gesture against patriarchy, whilst holding onto their sexual prowess as if to affirm: it is not necessary to give up on one's sexuality to have ambitions and agency in the outside world. Such a comment seems obvious and unnecessary, but in the context of recent developments it is crucial to re-iterate. In addition, I have selected here work that might be known to the reader outside the academy, work that has broken into the cinema's mainstream and in which women have had key creative roles as writers, producers and performers. The representation is important but who is in charge of telling the story is arguably more important.

There are a number of reflections one could offer in connection with the famous exchange between Trump and Clinton, not least the fact that a year after the presidential campaign a new trauma swept Western culture: the sexual harassment scandal of Harvey Weinstein and many women he preyed upon, followed by the '#MeToo' campaign on social media,[7] which gained millions of followers in a matter of days in the autumn of 2017 – almost exactly a year after the infamous 'nasty woman' comment. The '#MeToo' campaign encouraged women to post on Twitter and Facebook an admission that we have had a personal experience of sexual harassment, or, to put it differently, the

'#MeToo' campaign insisted on as many women as possible recognising their personal knowledge of what it feels to be treated like a sex object without wishing to be one.[8] It is important to bear in mind that the Weinstein scandal takes place at the heart of Hollywood, the dream factory that still produces the most influential cinema globally. What does it say about the production of cinema today when the allegations of misconduct appear to be rippling through the film industry both in the United States and elsewhere? What chances are there for a sustained change in both the representation of women in cinema and also the handing over the reins of creative power to women in any meaningful way? These are not the questions I will be attempting to answer in this monograph; nonetheless they are worth posing. However much we all would love to declare ourselves 'nomads' focusing on 'becoming' and fluidity, borrowing from Rosi Braidotti's *Nomadic Theory* (2011), pulling down binaries of body and soul, man and woman, and different ethnicities, a position not easily adoptable in this day and age quite yet. It is important to hold onto the vision, though, as an aspirational utopia and a model for thinking rather than being in the world. It is too early to give up on the nastiness.

Braidotti would like us to re-think our reasoning about the world in term of dislodging the dominance of the 'majority' which she does define as human, white and male:

> Nomadic thought opposes to this an ethics of qualitative transformation and a politics of complexity and affirmation. By extension, this scheme also implies various empirical minorities (women, blacks, natives, animals, plants, seeds, and molecules etc.) are the privileged starting point for active and empowering processes of becoming.
>
> (2011: 29–30)

The project requires a profound re-thinking of identity and in a way memory and history if it is to be taken seriously. She sees this male oriented identity as not only flawed but simply an obstacle to a further development of identities. She writes about 'a nomadic, nonlinear philosophy of time' (ibid.: 31) which will encompass 'internally fractured coalitions of subjects-in-becoming' (ibid.: 31). This idea of collations and allegiances – including inter-species allegiances – is echoed in the work of Donna Haraway and other post-humanist thinkers. In our intellectual journeys in this book our guiding light is a conviction and a hope that a cultural change is possible and will take place, or rather is taking place – but it is possible that in this transitional period in which our killjoyness and nastiness is a necessary quality that engenders change.

However much I personally believe in 'intimate connections between critique and creativity' (ibid.: 32), however much it is very clear that many men are better feminists than some women, and the recognition of gender fluidity a significant step forward in the contemporary world, the simple fact is that the battle for power in society and culture cannot be declared fought and won. The nasty woman is a warrior in this battle, she gets things wrong, she suffers and causes suffering as she seeks news way of being represented in cinema – and elsewhere. The nasty woman would like not to be nasty but she does want not to be a 'cool girl' any more, the category invented, or perhaps just named by Gillian Flynn in *Gone Girl*, of a (young) woman who is game for anything, and who is prepared to be everything that a man wants her to be without putting any demands on him at all. The cool girl is good looking, charming, thin, well educated, a professional who cooks a fabulous meal and gives a perfect blow job, who is innocent but adventurous and also endlessly supportive and forgiving. She is an impossible patriarchal fantasy pretending to be a post-feminist success. The 'cool girl' is also the perfect housewife in Chantal Akerman's classic feminist film *Jeanne Dielman* (1975) who performs all the mundane womanly tasks perfectly until one day she can do so no more and, without a word of explanation, she kills a man.

Figure 0.1 The 'perfect housewife' (Delphine Seyrig) in *Jeanne Dielman* (Chantal Akerman 1975)

Might this also be the cool girl – the girl who puts up with abuse before finally raising the alarm and speaking up? In some films, she does more than speak – she enacts a metaphorical revenge against patriarchy, which really is very violent and clearly needs further re-thinking and re-imagining for, as a proposition, this will not take us very far.

It is for that reason that the '#MeToo' campaign and the 'nasty woman' phrase are worth holding in one space. The new film based on the actual experiences of the documentary filmmaker Jennifer Fox, entitled *The Tale* (2018) with Laura Dern, brings up the issue of abuse and consent, reminding us that there are moments when the consent is but a delusional acquiescence to patriarchal power, a Stockholm syndrome of sorts often imbued by a skewed power balance. This is not to be prudish or limiting but it is a simple and unfortunate fact of life, clinically and philosophically supported, beginning with by the Freudian and Lacanian notion of transference, through Judith Butler's *Psychic Life of Power* (1997) to various contemporary accounts of abuse which at the time might have appeared to have been a seduction.[9]

For me personally these discussions have brought back some memories I would rather not remember, which I am bracketing here simply not to clutter my argument (and the '#MeToo' stories, including my own, are frankly painfully tedious in their predicted repetitiveness). The two campaigns also reminded me how 'the nasty woman' and the '#MeToo' are in some way connected, or can be.

Medusa, sexual violations and mad nasty women

If one considers the famous nasty women in the Metropolitan Museum tour, the figure of Medusa is one that features extensively. Medusa is the archetypal creature who started out as beautiful and pure, serving in Athena's temple in Greek antiquity but was sexually assaulted and lost everything even as she gained an unusual power over men. She was raped by Poseidon and lost her innocence. Much has been written about Medusa by Romantic (male) poets. Goethe, Shelley, Rosetti, Swinburne all had their own take on this tale, focusing more on the elements of storytelling and poetry rather than the gender narrative, whilst more recent feminist writers such as Helen Cixous, Teresa de Lauretis (1984) and Diana Fuss began to re-write the myth.[10]

Athena, herself a pretty nasty woman par excellence (the goddess of war in antiquity), in a rage at having her temple desecrated by Poseidon's rape of Medusa, makes her into a creature which any man must fear forever: she is monstrous, she freezes men with her gaze and kills innocent sailors. It is fascinating to consider that in the myth Athena chooses to make the victim of rape into a tool of her fury, thus punishing the latter too – Medusa gains immeasurable power but of course she loses herself, she forever loses who she is: the sexual assault evokes rage but is also destructive to the one who suffers it. There is something painful in the story and its fascination goes beyond the myth, for clearly it touches both on the fear of the sexual violation and the inevitable loss that it carries with itself once experienced by a woman.[11]

At this moment in time, significantly, the women who brought their accusations against Weinstein and others have been believed in stark contrast to various other instances when they were not. Nonetheless, quite quickly, almost immediately, the woman who began the disclosures, Rose McGowan, was indeed named as 'nasty' in various media and social media outlets; she was accused of allegedly demanding money for her assaults and only going after Harvey Weinstein in this public way after it was professionally profitable for her to do so or after he declined the money she had tried to extort from him – a claim which has been refuted in various statements that followed.[12] Yet, it is clear that niceness is not only overrated but can be a dangerous proposition, for it can lead to tactical compliance (to get jobs or favours) which turns into complicity with conservative patriarchal systems.

There is something else here to pause over and consider: women are still viewed as suspicious when they name their abusers and fight back. Apart from the mythical creatures, stories and fairytales, there is a history of the 'nasty woman' in Western history who becomes 'nasty' as a response to a sexual violation or a violation of some other kind perpetrated by men. One of the most famous 'nasty women' in the history of art was Artemisia Gentileschi (born around 1590) a late Renaissance / Baroque painter, a daughter of a famous artist Orazio whose associate Agostino Tassi, another quite well-known painter *and* her tutor, raped her brutally when she was a young girl and indeed his pupil (Bal 2006). Artemisia insisted on pressing charges – a gesture which was completely unheard of at the time. What ensued was a celebrated trial in which Artemisia was discredited in every possible way, called 'insatiable whore' and worse. She was tortured during the trial in order to find out whether she was 'lying'. The rapist was finally sent to prison for one year and Artemisia was seen by her contemporaries as 'monstrous' – both because of the scandal but also because of her talent and industrious commitment to her work, to her art, despite the obstacles. She was strange, her strength and tenacity perceived as 'inhuman'. Famously, she painted at least two different versions of the notorious biblical tale of Judith cutting of the head of Holofernes – the second one even more brutal and bloody than the first one: a case of extraordinary sublimation, if one ever doubted the creative links between trauma and creativity as presented by Freud and Lacan.[13]

The remarkable fact of the Artemisia story is that, despite her extraordinary artistry, she is not well known – her sexual history, the scandal, her reputation for being 'nasty' translated itself into centuries of scholarly suspicion and neglect. Why was her extraordinary genius overlooked, now cry the scholars and the critics? Why? Because for centuries she has been perceived as a nasty woman, and her art therefore not really worth examining per se.[14]

At the same time pretty much as the scandals in Italy and Artemisia's trial, Shakespeare (1564–1616) wrote a number of plays in which women feature extensively. In terms of the nasty woman and the forerunner of a *femme fatale* we have Lady Macbeth, but there is also of course Kate in *The Taming of the Shrew* who indeed is tamed comprehensively, and even though love appears to be her reward, one has suspicions whether the writer had a more basic agenda of presenting the necessity of succumbing to the patriarchal rules of female behaviour at the time. *Hamlet*'s Ophelia and her madness and its disruptive and nasty quality has been the subject of a multitude of interpretations both in terms of theatrical ones as well as literary and academic ones. The work of Elaine Showalter (1985) offers extraordinarily detailed surveys of different approaches to the character of Ophelia – including to her mind the unsatisfactory psychoanalytical interpretations. What is interesting, however, is how much Showalter feels the representation of Ophelia's madness corresponded to the documented insanity of the 19th century hysterics whose voice became the subject of multiple feminist re-interpretations. The nastiness of these women was connected to their bodies, their sexuality and the unfulfilled and often repressed sexual desire, with their agency still thwarted.

The 'nasty woman' who becomes nasty after traumatic love experiences, sexual violations and disappointments, and who is driven to madness by men, is a trope that becomes a very popular and familiar one in Gothic novels, including those written by women in late 18th, 19th and early 20th centuries. The notion of insanity or hysteria, which might appear a way out of the patriarchal system, has been prevalent throughout the 19th and 20th centuries with works such as Horace Walpole's

The Castle of Otranto (1764), Walter Scott's *The Bride of Lammermoor* (1819), Ann Radcliffe's *The Mysteries of Udolpho* (1794), Jane Austen's *Northanger Abbey* (1817) and Emily Bronte's *Wuthering Heights* (1847). The heroines in these novels are usually stripped of their agency in the main narrative of the story and their nastiness becomes a desperate gesture that usually leads to their death – not as a conscious sacrifice but rather as an inevitable consequence of their madness. The Medusa syndrome is replicated here as men in these stories often get punished too by the wronged women – usually once it is too late to look for any more creative and positive solutions. The message conveyed by these works is clear: any gesture against the heteronormative ideals is a super risky affair and will leave the one who attempts it totally disempowered and probably dead before long.

In addition, there are then stories and indeed operas in which the nasty and fallen woman in the form of various courtesans moves away from her position of some power over men (be it through her sexuality) to a position of sacrifice and a necessary death (to atone for her nastiness) – the famous and influential novella by Alexandre Dumas in *The Lady of the Camellias* (*La Dame aux Camelias*) (1848), then made into numerous theatre adaptations and then the famous opera by Verdi, *La Traviata* (1852) are but some examples. It was also the subject of multiple film and television adaptations – the public taste for a tale of a fallen woman redeemed by love but still having to be punished is quite remarkable. Puccini's *La Boheme* has a nasty fallen woman too who is redeemed in her sacrifice for the man she loves. The death of the woman, nasty and tainted despite her newly attained purity, is obviously a necessary quality of this work. This trope was very popular in early cinema too, in films starring Pola Negri such as *Mania* (1918), *Madam Du Barry* (1919), *Das Martyrium* (1921) and others. Another fantasy of a nasty woman who tries to defy the patriarchal order only to be killed by a betrayed lover is George Bizet's *Carmen* (1875) (based on a story of the same name written by Prosper Mérimée, which indeed became one of Pola Negri's great roles in 1920). We love Carmen stating boldly to Don José, who at this point is her husband – and not just a lover any more: 'I don't want to be harassed and above all I don't want anyone telling me what to do. I want to be free and do what I like' (Mérimée 1980: 95). But, it is very clear that her (sexual) freedom cannot last and her way of living is doomed: Don José begs her to give it up but she, Antigone-like, refuses and so has to die: nastiness does not pay in the patriarchal world.

The trope continues: a woman who falls out of a sexual harness of marriage will have to be punished sooner rather than later, the narrative of her story put on display for public enjoyment on the one hand and as a warning on the other.

Female voices and female subjectivity

Kaja Silverman (1988) suggested almost 30 years ago that the issues of male and female subjectivity in cinema and elsewhere are deeply linked to the voice with which they speak – figuratively and literally: whereas 'male subjectivity is most fully realized [. . .] when it is least visible [. . .] female subjectivity is most fully achieved [. . .] when it is most visible' (Silverman 1988: 164). She adds: 'the crucial project with respect to the female voice is to find a place from which it can speak and be heard, not to strip it of discursive rights' (ibid.: 192). The notion of finding one's voice and holding onto it is a key notion not only in feminism but in life – perhaps for everybody but for a woman in particular.

The notion of how exactly this could be achieved and what it might mean is a moot point. In terms of the writing, and in particular academic writing, this might mean allowing oneself to be more clearly visible in the work. This is the project that, whilst obvious, still seems deeply controversial in the academy. First of all, the notion of the 'voice': what is and where are the boundaries of our personal and our academic and professional personas? The '#MeToo' campaign brought into focus the truth that for women certainly these boundaries can indeed be fluid and that making them rigid can be a retroactive and conservative step. Somehow though, bringing one's own emotions and personal experience into a serious discourse is still viewed with deep suspicion, and even for feminist writers opinion remains divided. My personal experience is not part of this book, although on rare occasions I have brought it into this volume, but at all times I speak from a position of a woman filmmaker and an interdisciplinary scholar. The voices of the artists I feature speak in ways that define the subjectivity of their characters who often break the accepted canons of storytelling (the long sex scene in *Red Road* (2006), the fake archive in *Stories We Tell* (2012), or the mixing of genres in *Gone Girl*) but mostly their voices are seen in the creation of the lead female character, a different kind of 'nasty woman' – a neo *femme fatale* who is not punished in the storyworld of the work for her transgressions. She does not die. I will repeat this statement throughout the second half of this Introduction, for this is a crucial and new point: the nasty woman lives and triumphs.

In her discussion of female authorship, Catherine Grant (2000) mentions importantly the fact that the notion of female authorial authority was ignored by early feminist theorists, perhaps also because there was not much of the actual film production created by women. Grant reminds us of Johnston's (1973) early statement that 'The image of women in the cinema has been an image created by men' (Johnston, quoted in Grant 2000). The emergence of women's cinema has begun the transformation of that image. Johnston saw women's cinema as a potentially *counter cinema* which, at the time of her writing, was not yet a realised possibility. Johnston wanted future feminist filmmaking to learn from these examples of entertainment films, 'in which the feminine "voice", by formal means, breaks through (ruptures) the patriarchal discourse', as Janet Bergstrom noted (1988: 81). Whilst attempting new ways of thinking with and about the notion of female voice, this book is inspired by the current work on female authorship in film such as the work of Lucy Bolton, Sophie Mayer, Tanya Horeck, Ara Osterwell, Davina Quinlivan as well as the continuing presence in my mind of Elizabeth Cowie and Emma Wilson and so many others mentioned throughout this work.

The films I discuss in this volume offer a glimpse into contemporary English-speaking films with a nasty woman in the foreground. They have ambitions to be more than counter cinema: they have either broken into the mainstream (*Zero Dark Thirty* (2012), *Gone Girl, Girl on The Train*) or have gained very significant recognition at film festivals (*Red Road, Stories We Tell*). These are stories made by women about nasty women – and these voices matter and are assimilated into cinema and culture. All the characters in the films I present here indeed do break a number of patriarchal codes: they are not only pro-active, they often deploy dubious means to achieve their goals, they appear unmarried, and if they are married they subvert and undermine the whole idea of the patriarchal institution of marriage. It is very clear that the nasty woman emerges in different parts of the global cinema too and will need a further interrogation in due course. This book constitutes the first step to put the nasty woman firmly on our scholarly map as a category to be reckoned with.

The Trump/Clinton 'nasty woman' exchange and the '#MeToo' campaign signal an undeniable fact that for some men, decades after the first and second wave of feminism, in the sphere of the political and cultural life, when power is at stake, the gender of their opponent is evoked immediately as a marker of inferiority. Whilst clearly this is a disappointing stance, one has to accept that a certain amount of 'nastiness' may still have to be necessary in dealing with certain kinds of men in the patriarchal world we still live in. It is of course a leap to take a phrase from an actual political world to the world of cinema and fiction where characters are not real people but textual inventions brought to life by their creators. Nonetheless the 'nasty woman', as a concept, offers a pretext for reflecting on the development of the female character in contemporary cinema: the characters discussed in this book clearly belong to fictional systems and storyworlds. They are not real people – nonetheless, they have a 'symbolic effectiveness' that organises our everyday experience, making it appear coherent and intelligible. They also represent a step forward towards imagining a world in which women take power without having to 'lean in', using the expression by one of the most successful women in the contemporary corporate world, Cheryl Sandberg (2013), which fundamentally advocates working within the patriarchal structures for one's benefit, rather than fighting them on all fronts.[15]

The following chapters in this book unashamedly celebrate feminist and female authorship. As mentioned previously, the films discussed here have been directed, and often written, directed *and* produced, by a woman. 'Almost', as there is one exception to this rule, Chapter 2 on David Fincher's *Gone Girl* and Tate Taylor's *The Girl on The Train*. However, these two films are based on novels and then screenplays written by women (Gillian Flynn, Paula Hawkins and Erin Cressida Wilson). In that chapter I investigate in particular the contradictory narrative journeys that the characters are put on: Amy in *Gone Girl* arguably becomes a very nasty woman not only because of her pathological psychological make up, but also because of the structural patriarchal influences she has to deal with all her life. Rachel in *The Girl on the Train* is the only character whose personal narrative is presented in the film; she moves from the nasty woman to a different kind of a person who does not buy into the patriarchal narrative but ultimately seeks an alliance with another woman. Amy in *Gone Girl* arguably offers the clearest alternative to a traditional *femme fatale*, holding onto her defining characteristics of being a deceitful person whose sexuality can be used to dubious ends. The big difference is that her internal narration and the critique of the 'cool girl' give a clear rationale for her conduct – however brutal and pathological it is. She also survives and holds onto her power intact by the end of the film. *Girl on The Train* is interesting in its attempt to arrive at a very difficult alliance between two women who perceive each other as rivals. As such it marks an important alternative solution in the narrative offered. It is also worth observing in passing that the Western cultural canon, with its myths, legends and fairytales, does not provide a plethora of archetypal female collaborations or support for each other in stark contrast to endless tales of women competing with each other for male attention and a structural positioning of getting power through marriage and sexual privilege.

However much some women thinkers in non-Western cultures criticise feminism, it still remains the only movement defining female solidarity as the only viable force forward against the patriarchal might.

My discussion of *Gone Girl* will also engage with classic psycho-analytical film theory, drawing from Laura Mulvey's (1975) psycho-analytically fuelled ground-breaking discussion of the gaze vis-à-vis cinema's construction of the image of the woman, as well as Elizabeth Cowie's (1993, 1997) thinking about the woman as a sign. In *Gone Girl* Amy enacts within its narrative the cinema's construction of the image of woman on two occasions: firstly, Amy is literally turned into an image, in the storybooks her parents author, secondly, in her own invention as 'the cool girl' manufactured in order to please the men she encounters, and in particular Nick, and finally when she reinvents herself after five years of marriage. I am also interested in the function of the 'gaze' in relation to the gaze in the archetypal narratives – Medusa and Antigone. In the Medusa fable, her beauty attracts the gaze of the intruder and she is raped. It is of course that gaze, the gaze of a male explorer, that becomes his doom, following Athena's curse, as he gets struck by Medusa's gaze. The second archetype, that of Antigone, which I will discuss directly, and her determination and fate is also connected to her gaze, although clearly all three Lacanian registers (the Real, the Imaginary and the Symbolic) are deployed in the re-telling of the story by Lacan in his Seminar VII (on ethics) (Lacan 1986, 1992).

Antigone's forced choice is a response to the immovability of the male ruler but her decision is connected to her gaze, to the language and finally to her body: she sees the dead brother, she is forbidden through language to fulfil her promise and the rule of the ancient law and so she has to be prepared to sacrifice her body – and those of others. But the driver, which sets the story in motion, is indeed her gaze – the act of seeing.

In *Gone Girl* there are perhaps two decisive moments that activate Amy's narrative: when Amy decides she is not loved anymore as she *sees* her husband having an affair with a younger woman; then, unexpectedly, she falls in love with him after *seeing* him interviewed on television (as he lies about his love for her). The other characters under discussion too begin to become nasty and 'monstrous' when they are pushed beyond what they can put up with – and this takes place when they *see* things: Jackie in *Red Road seeing* Clive on the surveillance screens; Maya in *Zero Dark Thirty seeing* her best friend being blown up on computer screens; Rachel in *Girl on the Train seeing* the fantasy of the happy families from the train, etc. In *Stories We Tell* the filmmaker controls our gaze, in her presenting the fake obsolete archive of her childhood.

In *Gone Girl, The Girl on the Train, Red Road* and *Zero Dark Thirty* the act of looking and seeing is the driving force that transforms the nice girl into the nasty woman. This is very different from the traditional *femme fatale*, whose driving force is the man's arrival on the scene. The 'nasty woman' of the neo *femme fatale* is not dissimilar to a *femme fatale* but she is *not* a *femme fatale*: her determination might be immoral too but it is ethical – at least within Lacanian/Antigonian terms. I will discuss it in the ensuing section.

Antigone: the archetypal 'nasty woman' without the sexual violation

Lacan interpreted Sophocles' Antigone in his Seminar VII (*The Ethics of Psychoanalysis*) (1986, 1992). Antigone is the protagonist of Sophocles' play written in 441 BC about the daughter of Oedipus who disobeys the current ruler of her kingdom, Creon, as she insists on performing several times the act of burial of her deceased brother Polyneices, knowing as she does that the act will evoke fury of Creon and will result in her certain death. In the event, despite the repeated and increasingly desperate pleas of her family, including her sister Ismene and fiancée Haemon (who happens to be Creon's son) she carries on with the repeated attempts to bury her brother; her punishment is to be buried alive in a cave. When Creon changes his mind too late and breaks the entrance to the cave, Antigone is found already dead, having committed suicide, presumably choosing her agency again over a slow and painful death by starvation. As a direct result of her actions, her fiancée commits suicide too as does his mother. Creon is a broken man and the whole kingdom is left in ruins.

Antigone, her dazzling beauty in her determination to do the thing she is committed to, has fascinated scholars, poets and writers for centuries. She has been appropriated by the feminist icon Luce Irigaray (1985, 1991, 2010) and the radical thinker Judith Butler (2003).[16] Bonnie Honig, in her fascinating book *Antigone Interrupted* (2013), offers both a review of the scholarly work to date on Antigone as well as her own interpretations of what she might mean in the history of ideas and defiant stances against male authority. The heroines in the films I have mentioned previously, through their nastiness, offer a rupture too – offering a clear and unambiguous departure from the previous status quo. Their agency and determination would render them 'ethical' in the Lacanian system – despite the deeds they commit.

My theorisation of the 'nasty woman', an alternative to Medusa's gaze, begins with the Lacanian notion of the ethical act consisting of 'not giving up on one's desire' and, once the commitment is made, to be able to be faithful to it 'beyond the limit' as Lacan puts it (Lacan [1959–60] 1992: 305) or 'to the end' in Žižek's words (1989).

I argue therefore that Antigone can be seen as a prototype of a beautiful 'nasty woman', perhaps alongside the figure of the monstrous Medusa, who remains connected to the hysteric. Antigone is driven to her nastiness by not giving up on her desire. Interestingly too, Antigone's strength is *not* related to her own sexuality (although one could argue, and Judith Butler does, that the incest and deep sexual transgression haunts this story through the line of Oedipus). In fact, one could argue that her renunciation of sexuality is necessary in her ascent to power. The virginal powerful (and often nasty) woman with historical and fictional female characters (such as Elizabeth I or Joan of Arc for example) offers a way of being which many contemporary women might find unappealing. It is interesting to consider that her sacrifice became a necessary component of her fidelity to Antigone's commitment – it was not a result of insanity or a hysterical momentary loss of control. It would have been perfectly possible for Antigone to live were it not for Creon's insistence on his dictum. The sacrifice is a choice that only became necessary in the face of patriarchal rigidity.[17]

A *femme fatale* does not choose sacrifice most of the time, not the one that would involve her in any event. She appears to like sex and uses her sexuality to achieve her goals. I say 'appears' as it is only in *Red Road* that the she truly embraces its transformative power, for herself, but in ways that benefit the world in which she lives. It is also that film which re-defines the notion of punishment and revenge so prevalent in the classic *femme fatale*.

Neo *femme fatale*

I define the 'nasty woman' in this book as a partial descendant of the well-known figure of the *femme fatale* in *film noir*. The *femme fatale* is one of the original, powerful 'nasty woman' figures in cinema and much has been written about her, about whether she is but a male fantasy or whether she might be relevant to contemporary feminism (see, for example Bronfen 2004; Doane 1987, 1991; Copjec 1993, and many others). She is usually immoral and beautiful. Both as a male fantasy and as a representation of female power, she holds endless appeal, which I would argue, originates not only from her sexuality and beauty, but because she offers a way out of the rigid patriarchal systems of power and authority – which are also tediously restricting even for those who benefit from these conservative patterns – namely men.

In the heyday of *femme fatales* in the 1940's (in films such as, for example, *Double Indemnity* (1944) or *The Postman Always Rings Twice* (1946)), she might have been the sole figure fracturing male dominance in Hollywood narratives – but she was allowed to do so ONLY very briefly – for the spectator's fun, before being disempowered. Traditionally, this transient fantasy is immediately exposed as 'nasty' – it is far too dangerous to let a character who manipulates men live her independent life – and so she is usually killed off (a trope very familiar from the Gothic novels and operas mentioned before), or perhaps occasionally gets domesticated. A *femme fatale*'s brief transgression in the original form is never allowed to survive in these classic works. It is a crucial point to consider here: the new *femme fatale* is nasty and Maya of *Zero Dark Thirty*, Amy of *Gone Girl,* Jackie of *Red Road*, and Rachel of *The Girl on The Train* for different reasons come to a point where indeed like Antigone, they become (as Lacan reminds us after Sophocles) 'monstrous', 'inflexible', 'inhuman' – and yet their commitment to the chosen path *outside* the conventional patriarchal systems could also be described as full of dignity and beauty. Nasty women and *femme fatales* do not give up on their desire – no matter what. The difference between the story of Antigone and the narratives of these contemporary films and the neo *femme fatales* created by female writers and directors is that they do not perish. A sacrifice is often called for and delivered – but not the final one.

Neo *femme fatale* versus the nasty woman

I see this project as the beginnings of a discussion of the 'nasty woman' in cinema and culture rather than a definitive statement on it. This book recognises that the nasty woman can also be an action woman or an older woman or a lesbian woman – but these, as previously stated, are bracketed in this project. For the purposes of this book the nasty woman is still recognisably a *new femme fatale* with some additional different traits – most importantly she survives. She lives on. She emerges triumphant. She is also conceived, as previously stated, by a woman writer or director.

In her recent book, Katherine Farrimond (2017) offers a comprehensive summary of the scholarship pertaining to the figure of the *femme fatale* in American cinema. Here though, building on this feminist scholarship, I offer further ways of thinking about the 'nasty woman' and a *neo femme fatale*, including female characters in films which would not usually be a part of the *femme fatale* discussion: that is to say, films which have the elements of the nastiness and *femme fatalness* but not in an obvious way. In my selection of films, I have included a documentary *Stories We Tell* (2012) made by a woman (Sarah Polley) about her quest to establish truth about her mother's relationship to her father and the truth about her own family relationships. In the course of the film, she chooses to be quite 'nasty', with her ruthless pursuit of the project, with her lack of great concern for the hurt she will inevitably cause to her family as well as with her choice of the cinematic method, which fundamentally deceives the viewer. I argue that her nastiness is a necessary tool in her project to re-gain the power which her mother lost forever to various men she loved, including the filmmaker's father.

Psychoanalysis, as a theoretical way of thinking about the world and a clinical practice, has significantly contributed to the debates about power balance both in terms of being seen as a proponent of dominant thinking but also as a way of questioning the unknown, the Other inside us, and therefore, which by definition dislodges the rigid, the known and unmovable, the patriarchal in short. However, I do point out its severe limitations, in particular regarding the deployment of the Oedipal story as a serious model of relationships between people. In my discussion of *Gone Girl* in particular, I take issue with the readings of *Blue Velvet* (1986) by psychoanalytically influenced feminist scholars. Taking psychoanalysis too rigidly can lead to a re-inscription of the patriarchal, rather than its demolition.

One of the ongoing debates in feminist scholarship in general and in feminist scholarship about the cinema in particular, has been the relationship between feminine subjectivity and the body, the language and the power (or absence of it) of a woman in a patriarchal system. A discussion regarding the use of psychoanalysis and the haptic film theory (Sobchack 2004) is worth noting here. Some scholars disavow it completely, others find combining the two helpful (Wilson 2012; Quinlivan 2012, 2015; Marks 1998, for example). The combining of documentary and fiction in one conceptual space too has been developed by feminist scholars (Wilson 2012; Quinlivan 2015: 17) and this is the work I build on here as well, drawing from a variety of cultural inspirations.

In connection with the 'nasty woman' and a *neo femme fatale*, it is the figure of a female hysteric who connects to the insane women of the Gothic novels mentioned previously. A hysteric, with her theatricality, her bodily performance, her gesture of both a protest and a demand, is something that echoes the tragedy of Medusa who becomes deadly after her profound violation. Psychoanalysis did not attempt to connect the archetypal figure of Medusa to that of the hysteric. The suffering and the unfairness of the figure is not discussed – a possibility of Athena playing a brutal mother, in the psyche of a hysteric is ignored despite, to my mind, its fairly obvious potential for such an interpretation. The inability to express the profound pain, the perceived monstrosity of the victim, her condemnation to a life of horror through being an executioner of the lost men, and never their lover – all of these possibilities are disavowed in the classic psychoanalytical reading.

In a very short piece on Medusa, Freud focused on her castrating abilities and the pictorial snakes reminding him of the hair (which to my mind again is a stretch). And if indeed she does represent the boy's fear of being castrated, then perhaps the boy might like to grow up before it is too late and become more accepting of alternative solutions which may not include a castration ('when a boy, who has hitherto been unwilling to believe the threat of castration, catches the sight of female genitals, probably those of an adult, surrounded by hair, and essentially those of his mother' (Freud 1997: 264)).

In her re-telling of the case of one of the hysterics, namely Anna O., Colette Soler (2006) recalls the bizarre tale of Breuer falling into transferential love with Anna O. without recognising the process, and completely losing his professional cool when he learnt that his patient not only relapsed dramatically after his departure, but moreover had a hysterical phantasmatic experience of giving birth. Perhaps the gaze of the hysteric did temporarily leave Breuer castrated and petrified – in a painful episode of the clinical practice. Soler draws our attention to the real Anna O. who re-emerges as a fully engaged member of society doing important social work in exotic places under her real name (ibid: 4–6). It is not clear (despite the claims of Freud et al) whether the extraordinary encounter with the petrified Dr Breuer did contribute to her cure – it might well have done, although the curious abandoning of her in the middle of the treatment appears a cruel if understandable move. It is almost amusing to note that Freud does not record the inherent issues in the treatment of Anna O. – her torment and Breuer's confusion temporarily written out of the mainstream history of the practice. But the shades of the archetypal panic over the strength of the insane woman's desire so well known from the Gothic novels, are indeed visible in this case study. Perhaps an experience of love, be it brief and indeed phantasmatic, was enough for this particular person to find her place in the Symbolic. Perhaps all she needed was to talk to somebody who appeared to listen – for a while. Perhaps the shock of being abandoned was enough to make her go into the world and do work devoted indeed to women in trouble in different continents (Soler 2006: 6). Nonetheless, one thing is clear: her strength and resolve appear to have overcome her passionate dependency on the man who may have helped her too. These tendencies stand firm between her Death Drive and her creativity. They do in the end flow Antigone-like from her own desire and she succeeds in the external world, in the Symbolic – alone but victorious and not mad. That hysteric-turned-proactive creative figure who does survive her insanity without succumbing to her body or her mind, or the patriarchal, gives us a structure for a new narrative.

We can spot the shades of this kind of 'modified hysteric', a hysteric who combines her furious frustration with a cool Antigone-like determination, in all the heroines of the films discussed in this book. The suffering and the physical ailments of the hysterics, their lack and in some way weakness, is replaced by a more resolute nastiness: the melancholia of Jackie in *Red Road* progresses to a determinedly nasty agency which the filmmaker then is bold enough to transform into something else again, namely the life-giving erotic agency of her subject; the promiscuity of the mother in *Stories We Tell* is replaced by her daughter's creative and brutal single mindedness; the psycho-sociopathic traits of Amy in *Gone Girl* are a defensive presentation of a revenge against patriarchal violence – a metaphor which re-defines the subject; the alcoholism of Rachel in *The Girl on the Train* begins to give way to a determined seeking of the truth; and the almost autistic single mindedness of Maya in *Zero Dark Thirty* which delivers a result nobody else could do. In the construction of the characters and the stories by the female auteurs, their steadfastness is not that of a helpless hysteric ready to perish but rather is that of a powerful descendant of Antigone, quite 'nasty' but also perhaps commanding respect if not affection on the part of the viewer.

The voices of the women in the films I discuss here are very singular and clearly feminine in a particular way: they are full of agency to the end. Despite their nastiness their storyworlds begin to present alternative solutions – desired and expected by the third wave feminism, that is, attempts at building new allegiances with men, without buying into their patriarchal expectations. The binary of the traditional systems begin to break down. The films offer beginnings of a new way of communicating, including female sexuality (particularly clear in *Red Road*).

The project of building new allegiances is very much under construction here: all the nasty women in the films I discuss are still pretty much alone – the allegiances with the Other so far have not yet worked out, as closeness without the chains appears a big challenge – in the world and in the cinema of women.

I begin with Maya of *Zero Dark Thirty* – a nasty woman who is perhaps most like the classic figure of Antigone, also in the abandonment of her sexuality. Her work is her mission and her mission is to rid the world of Osama Bin Laden who in this structure functions as the ultimate evil patriarchal character. Her work is that of actively dealing with mourning and melancholia, a trauma induced by the tragic and epic events of 9/11, which re-defined the world in ways which we would rather not have to deal with but indeed which demand a daily re-definition of the appropriate response. One could argue that all the films in the book deal with a need to redress the acute sense of loss, on the part of the women in culture and society, the loss of power and control which perhaps never was, the loss of some kind of acquiescence to the system, the trauma of a realisation that the further fight is necessary and goes on, however much the nasty woman would rather be the charming nourishment giver. Instead, the bewildering battle for some kind of balance in the world carries on.

Notes

1 Here are the websites for the nasty woman tour: www.facebook.com/events/122789921576978/ and www.shadyladiestours.com/nasty-women-at-the-metropolitan/ (accessed on 29 November 2017).

2 So brilliantly discussed by Barbara Creed (1993) and Carol Clover (1992).

3 For example www.theguardian.com/us-news/2016/oct/07/donald-trump-leaked-recording-women (accessed 19 November 2017).

4 Caitlin Flanagan in a recent article suggested that, at the time, the whole Clinton sexual harassment scandal was deeply inconvenient for the feminist and liberals. The article here has been challenged on social media but it is still worth considering how Hillary Clinton had to ride her husband's sexual history which certainly was not greatly helpful in her presidential campaign: www.theatlantic.com/entertainment/archive/2017/11/reckoning-with-bill-clintons-sex-crimes/545729/ (accessed 19 November 2017).

5 Even the notion of gender performativity (Butler 1990, 1993) could be interpreted as advocating the abolishment of strict gender binaries. This is not a space for discussing queer theories or indeed Rosi Braidotti whom I mention in passing in the body of the Introduction. My position is emphatically not that of biological or essentialist mode but disavowing the obvious continuing gender power imbalance across cultures seems an unproductive stance.

6 Marina Warner has written a number of books on fairytales, including *Once Upon a Time: A Short History of Fairy Tale* (2014). In Zimbabwe, a country I have lived and worked in, researched and written about (Piotrowska 2017), there is a figure of 'nyanga' who in addition could be argued to be transgender, as this witch sort of character can be an woman – or a man – and who knows about unorthodox cures and magical properties. In the Zimbabwean feminist writer and filmmaker Tsitsi Dangerembga's short film *Kare Kare Zvako* (2004) (*Mother's Day*) – the mother of the house is killed in order to provide nourishment for the starving family. In the film, which is a controversial mixture of surrealism and African beliefs, the woman is then cooked and eaten up by her husband before returning as a ghost of vengeance, definitely a pretty nasty woman by then.

7 http://edition.cnn.com/2017/10/30/health/metoo-legacy/index.html (accessed 19 November 2017).

8 For more on the #MeToo campaign, see: www.theguardian.com/lifeand style/2017/oct/28/metoo-hashtag-sexual-harassment-violence-challenge-campaign-women-men (accessed 27 November 2017).

9 This includes the infamous seduced intern Monika Lewinsky when she recently discussed her relationship with President Clinton, putting a different slant onto it: www.vanityfair.com/style/2018/05/monica-lewinsky-on-her-disinvitation-debacle (accessed 17 June 2018).

10 See for example a discussion of different versions of the myth by different authors in *The Medusa Reader* (2003) edited by Marjorie Garber, William R Kenan and Nancy Vickers; or *Laughing with Medusa* (2006) edited by Vanda Zajko and Miriam Leonard (which includes psychoanalytical readings denoting male fears of castration by a powerful female gaze: ibid.: 121).

11 Elizabeth Johnston more recently and indeed in connection with the 2016 American campaign, points out that even in the recent cinematic outputs, such as the *Clash of the Titans* (2010), the aspect of the myth of Medusa being the victim of the rape is ignored entirely and she is purely an object of fury and hate with no consideration whatever given to her suffering. (Johnston 2016).

12 www.thegatewaypundit.com/2017/10/milo-issues-blistering-critique-rose-mcgowan-hollywood-reels-sexual-harassment-drama/ www.nytimes.com/2017/10/28/us/rose-mcgowan-harvey-weinstein.html (accessed 19 November 2017).

13 I discuss sublimation in some detail throughout the book. In essence, in psychoanalysis it is the sublimation of the sexual drive (or desire) into a creative activity. 'Sublimation is nonetheless satisfaction of the drive, without repression' (Lacan 1999: 165–166).

14 (www.arthistoryarchive.com/arthistory/baroque/Artemisia-Gentileschi.html (accessed 15 November 2017).

www.theguardian.com/artanddesign/2016/oct/05/artemisia-gentileshi-painter-beyond-caravaggio (accessed 16 November 2017).

www.nytimes.com/topic/person/artemisia-gentileschi (accessed 14 November 2017).

15 For a critical note on Sandberg's book see for example: www.huffingtonpost. com/vanessa-garcia/why-i-wont-lean-in_b_3586527.html (accessed 27 November 2017).

16 Whilst Irigaray finds Antigone more straightforwardly a feminist figure challenging the patriarchal might, Butler does focus on Antigone in her act transgressing both gender norms and kinship norms (2003: 6) and proposes that Antigone's act is 'contingency' and not 'an immutable necessity' (ibid.: 6).

17 It is nonetheless important to point out too that however personally I am fond of Antigone and her courage against the nonsense of the patriarchal might, and however much her death in the narrative can be defended in a number of ways (one suggested by me in the body of this chapter) from the point of view of the cinema influencing society as well as reflecting it, and the point of view of the neo *femme fatale*, it would definitely have been better if she did survive her ordeal.

Bibliography

Bal, M. (ed.) (2006) *The Artemisia files*. Chicago: University of Chicago Press.

Barker, J. (2009) *The tactile eye: Touch and the cinematic experience*. Berkeley: University of California Press.

Bergstrom, J. (1988) 'Enunciation and Sexual Difference', in Penley, C. (ed.), *Feminism and Film Theory*. London: BFI Publishing/Routledge. pp. 159–185.

Braidotti, R. (2011) *Nomadic Theory: The Portable Rosi Braidotti*. New York: Columbia University Press.

Bronfen, E. (2004) '*Femme fatale*: Negotiations of tragic desire', *New Literary History* 35 (1), pp. 103–116.

Butler, J. (1990) *Gender trouble: Feminism and the subversion of identity*. London and New York: Routledge.

Butler, J. (1993) *Bodies that matter: On the discursive limits of 'sex'*. London and New York: Routledge.

Butler, J. (1997) *The psychic life of power*. Stanford: Stanford University Press.

Butler, J. (2003) *Antigone's claim: Kinship between life and death*. New York: Columbia University Press.

Clinton, H.R. (2017) *What happened*. New York: Simon & Schuster.

Clover, C. (1992) *Men, women and chainsaws: Gender in modern horror film*. London: BFI.

Copjec, J. (ed.) (1993) *Shades of noir: A reader*. New York: Verso.

Cowie, E. (1993) 'Film noir and women', in Copjec, J. (ed.), *Shades of noir: A reader*. New York: Verso, pp. 121–166.

Cowie, E. (1997) *Representing the woman: Cinema and psychoanalysis*. London: Macmillan.

Creed, B. (1993) *The monstrous-feminine: Film, feminism, psychoanalysis*. London: Routledge.

De Lauretis, T. (1984) 'Desire in narrative', in *Alice doesn't: Feminism, semiotics, cinema*. Bloomington: Indiana University Press, pp. 103–157.

Doane, M.A. (1987) 'The woman's film: Possession and address', in Gledhill, C. (ed.), *Home is where the heart is: Studies in melodrama and the woman's film*. London: BFI, pp. 283–298.

Doane, M.A. (1991) *Femmes fatales: Feminism, film theory, psychoanalysis*. New York: Routledge.

Farrimond, K. (2017) *Contemporary femme fatale: Gender, genre and American cinema*. London and New York: Routledge.

Freud, S. (1997) *Writings on art and literature*. Stanford: Stanford University Press.

Garber, M., Kenan, W.R., and Vickers, N. (eds.) (2003) *The Medusa reader*. New York: Routledge.

Grant, C. (2000) 'Secret agents: Feminist theories of women's film authorship': https://catherinegrant.org/secret_agents/ (accessed 22 June 2018).

Gray, E. (2016) 'How "Nasty Woman" became a viral call for solidarity', *Huffington Post*, 21 October: www.huffingtonpost.co.uk/entry/nasty-woman-became-a-call-of-solidarity-for-women-voters_us_5808f6a8e4b02444efa20c92 (accessed 22 June 2018).

Honig, B. (2013) *Antigone interrupted*. Cambridge: Cambridge University Press.

Irigaray, L. (1985 [1971]) *The speculum of the other woman*. Translated by G.C. Gill. Ithaca: Cornell University Press.

Irigaray, L. (1991) 'Questions to Emmanuel Lévinas on the divinity of love', in Bernasconi, R., and Critchley, S. (eds.), *Re-reading Lévinas*. Translated by M. Whitford. London: Athlone Press, pp. 109–118.

Irigaray. L. (2010) 'Antigone: Between myth and history/antigone's legacy', In Wilmer, S. E., and Zukauskaite, A. (eds.), *Interrogating Antigone in Postmodern Philosophy and Criticism*. Oxford: Oxford University Press.

Irigaray, L., and Whitford, M. (eds.) (1997 [1991]) *The Irigaray reader*. Oxford: Blackwell.

Johnston, C. (ed.) (1973) *Notes on women's cinema*. London: Society for Education in Film and Television.

Johnston, E. (2016) 'The original "Nasty Woman"', *The Atlantic*, 6 November: www.theatlantic.com/entertainment/archive/2016/11/the-original-nasty-woman-of-classical-myth/506591/ (accessed 20 October 2017).

Lacan, J. (1986 [1959–60]) *Le séminaire. Livre VII: l'éthique de la psychanalyse*. Paris: Seuil.

Lacan, J. (1992 [1959–60]) *Seminar VII. The ethics of psychoanalysis 1959–1960*. Translated by D. Potter. London: Taylor and Francis, Routledge.

Lacan, J. (1999 [1975]) *Seminar XX. On feminine sexuality, the limits of love and knowledge*. Translated by B. Fink. London and New York: W. W. Norton.

Lévinas, E. (1981) *Otherwise than being*. Translated by A. Lingis. The Hague: Martinus Nijhoff Publishers.

Marks, L. U. (1998) 'Video haptics and erotics', *Screen* 39 (4), pp. 331–348.

Mérimée, P. (1980) *Carmen*. Paris: Bordas.

Metz, C. (1982) *Psychoanalysis and cinema: The imaginary signifier*. Translated by C. Britton, A. Williams, B. Brewster and A. Guzzetti. London: Macmillan.

Mulvey, L. (1975) 'Visual pleasure and narrative cinema', *Screen* 16 (3), pp. 6–18.

Piotrowska, A. (2017) *Black and white: Cinema, politics and the arts in Zimbabwe*. London: Routledge.

Quinlivan, D. (2012) *The place of breath in cinema*. Edinburgh: Edinburgh University Press.

Quinlivan, D. (2015) *Filming the body in crisis: Trauma, healing and hopefulness.* Basingstoke: Palgrave Macmillan.

Sandberg, C. (2013) *Lean in: Women, work, and the will to lead.* New York: Alfred A. Knopf.

Showalter, E. (1985) 'Representing Ophelia: Women, madness, and the responsibilities of feminist criticism', in Parker, P., and Hartman, G. (eds.), *Shakespeare and the question of theory.* London: Methuen, pp. 77–94.

Silverman, K. (1988) *The acoustic mirror: The female voice in psychoanalysis and cinema.* Bloomington: Indiana University Press.

Sobchack, V. (2004) *Carnal thoughts: Embodiment and moving image culture.* Berkeley: University of California Press.

Soler, C. (2006) *What Lacan said about women: A psychoanalytic study.* Translated by J. Holland. New York: Other Press.

Warner, M. (2014) *Once upon a time: A short history of fairy tale.* Oxford: Oxford University Press.

Wilson, E. (2012) *Love, mortality, and the moving image.* Basingstoke: Palgrave Macmillan.

Zajko, V., and Leonard, M. (eds.) (2006) *Laughing with Medusa: Classical myth and feminist thought.* Oxford: Oxford University Press.

Žižek, S. (1989) *The sublime object of ideology.* London: Verso.

1 *Zero Dark Thirty*

'War autism' or a Lacanian ethical act?

Introduction

This chapter looks at a film which already feels like it comes from a slightly different era, as it was made a few years ago by a woman who some call pretty nasty – although nobody doubts her extraordinary storytelling talents and agency in getting her films made.

Zero Dark Thirty (Bigelow 2012) is a controversial film. Most notably, it has been accused both in the popular press and in some scholarly reviewers of justifying torture during the enhanced interrogations scenes of suspected terrorists. In the UK, *The Guardian* led the campaign demolishing the film's intellectual credibility; for example, the articles by Glenn Greenwald (2012) and Slavoj Žižek (2013) display quite an extraordinary fury in their criticism of Bigelow's film and her main character. K. Austin Collins in *The Ringer* (2018) re-examined the backlash cycle five years later, stating:

> Was *Zero Dark Thirty* a nuanced apologia or merely a reckless one? (Its status as a political defence was generally taken for granted.) Suddenly, everybody was a sociopolitically minded movie critic. We've tended to think of this kind of pushback as an essential indicator of the now-common Oscar backlash cycle.

Collins' article evokes the debate around the veracity of the film and its position in culture and society. More than any other film in the last 10 years, *Zero Dark Thirty* demands to be treated as a substantial cultural and societal intervention, and not just a piece of entertainment. As such, it remains important and its place in the history of cinema and culture is assured. Most of the debates did not centre on the issue of gender but rather on the limits of what a filmmaker ought to consider a suitable way to go about making a film. Collins reminds us that:

> It had been revealed that the CIA had willingly cooperated and even collaborated with Bigelow and her screenwriting partner, Mark Boal, in the making of the movie. This news dropped thanks to a Freedom of Information Act request on behalf of the conservative group Judicial Watch, which acquired emails between Pentagon and White House officials discussing their involvement with the project.

The atmosphere of the filmmakers somehow collaborating with the regime of the day prevailed. Feminists attacked Bigelow for allegedly endorsing torture, with one of the most vociferous critics, Naomi Wolf in *The Guardian*, comparing the director to the Nazi propagandist Leni Riefensthal: 'Like Riefenstahl, you are a great artist. But now you will be remembered forever as torture's handmaiden' (Wolf 2013). Six years on K. Austin Collins repeats what I say in this chapter – that 'it's also difficult to take seriously the argument that representation is endorsement'. In the same article the author makes additional points which I develop in this chapter, namely that Bigelow really focuses on the central female character's determined pursuit, which is rather disturbing in its single mindedness:

> She's lost friends; she herself has survived a bombing and a barrage of bullets. And she's soaked it all up and thrown it back into her work. By the time all of this happens, the rhythmic back and forth between interrogation and reenactment has been broken, and all that is left is Maya, and her hunger. The hunt for bin Laden no longer feels like the ritualized misexecution of overwrought interrogation tactics. It is powered, instead, by a singular thirst for personal payback, proffered by a woman who, as the movie sees it, practically has to force the country's hand to get what she wants. President Obama, who hovers just outside the movie, never fully materializing, seems halfway reluctant. Maya is a zealot, by comparison.

It is my belief that the film did not justify torture but it is not what this essay centres on although I will touch upon the issue later on. The chapter focuses on the main character, Maya, and her 'hunger', her relationship to the events as they unfold. If we follow the two path classic approach suggested in the introduction of this volume, that is of Antigone on the one hand, and Medusa on the other, this piece of cinematic work focuses on the former trope. I aim here to discuss Maya's ultimate commitment to the project of capturing Osama bin Laden as presented in Kathryn Bigelow's film through the lens of the Antigone-like approach to the task. To present it further, I choose the Lacanian notion of the ethical act consisting of 'not giving up on one's desire' and, once the commitment is made, to be able to be faithful to it 'beyond the limit' as Lacan puts (Lacan [1959–60] 1992: 305) or – 'to the end' in Žižek's words (1989). I will also suggest that Maya's position is also a response to trauma, as, in a way, is that of Antigone, the protagonist under scrutiny in Lacan's Seminar VII on Ethics. Maya in many ways is a 'nasty woman' – she is intransigent, can be quite cruel and difficult. Collins (2018) calls Maya's determination a 'Sisyphean one-woman effort', also pointing out that 'She's a character defined by the singularity of her vision and effort, which makes it hard to see her as a metaphor for the rest of us. Maya is Maya' One could argue though – which I am doing in this chapter – that this nasty woman is not so much a metaphor for us all but instead a manifestation of a possible 'nasty' but effective stance vis-à-vis the world.

In connection with that I will engage, among other writings, with William Brown's (2013) discussion of the film and Maya's role in it. In his blog, in essence, Brown suggests that Maya's dogged determination to capture Bin Laden as presented in the film, and constructed as such by the director, is a form of autistic behaviour, characterised by a complete lack of empathy. He calls her behaviour and conduct 'war autism'. I will suggest that far from suffering from any kind of autism, metaphoric or otherwise, the film tracks Maya's metamorphosis from being a victim of the (patriarchal) system to acquiring agency and power of her own, be it within the limits of what she is allowed to choose. I also argue that Maya's position in this situation denotes an interruption and not an approval of patriarchal procedural systems that she is a part of.[1] Despite the fact that Maya's 'no' is aimed in the end mostly at shaking the immobilising procedures of the system run by male line managers, it is that 'no' which succeeds in delivering Bin Laden – and possibly restoring some kind of equilibrium in the world, like the act of Antigone, despite the violence inherent in both.

Neither Antigone nor Maya are straightforwardly 'good' in a way that would fit into Christian (or indeed Levinasian) systems being characterised by loving one's neighbour or by the Infinite Responsibility for the Other in Emmanuel Lévinas (1981). Here Maya, like Antigone, is indeed 'monstrous', 'inflexible', 'inhuman' – and yet her commitment to the chosen path is also full of dignity and beauty. I will suggest that the re-formulation of Lacan's ethics of desire by Alain Badiou offers a helpful theoretical paradigm with which to consider Maya's stance.

'Autistic' or 'not giving up on her desire'?

Brown refers to a number of autistic 'symptoms' as he sees them in the film, namely Maya's alleged inability to form eye contact with the people she encounters, for example, her friend and colleague, Jessica. He suggests that 'Bigelow's film may indeed normalize torture, as well as the mental conditions that allow it (i.e. a lack of empathy), and that this in turn may well influence audiences and their attitudes towards violence'. In order to substantiate his argument, Brown evokes well-known claims by neuroscientists and psychologists, particularly referencing Christian Keyesers who was one of the key figures in the discovery of mirror neurons, who describes his experience with an autistic man, Jerome, as involving Jerome always looking around the room but – significantly – 'never into my eyes' (Keysers 2011: 18, cited by Brown) and Simon Baron-Cohen, Britain's leading expert on autism. Brown cites the latter's suggestion that there are two stages to empathy: recognition and response. As Baron-Cohen says, 'both are needed, since if you have the former without the latter you haven't empathised at all' (Baron-Cohen 2011: 12). Brown claims that Maya shows neither. To my mind this is a very problematic trope indeed. Maya's actions do not stem from a lack of empathy but rather, if anything, directly from it, as I hope to demonstrate. Her determination, (no matter what), in Lacanian terms, is an ethical act. In order to discuss it theoretically, I now turn to Lacanian ethics of desire.

The ethics of desire

The issue of ethics versus desire in the work of Jacques Lacan is a complex matter but here I will contain the discussion to Seminar VII given in 1957 entitled The Ethics of Psychoanalysis. It is here we find Lacan's notorious and controversial notion: 'ne pas céder sur son désir'[2] translated as a confusing 'not to give ground relative to one's desire' (Lacan 1992 [1959–60]: 321). Zupančič (2000) and Žižek's (2005 [1994]) translate this instead as simply 'not giving up on one's desire' (Žižek 2005: 61).

At the heart of this discussion of ethics in Seminar VII, there is for Lacan the figure of Antigone (and not Oedipus – although he is mentioned) – the protagonist of Sophocles' play written in 441 BC about the daughter of Oedipus who disobeys the current ruler of her kingdom, Creon, as she insists on performing several times the act of burial of her deceased brother Polyneices, knowing as she does that the act will evoke fury of Creon and will result in her certain death. In the event, despite the pleas of her family, including her sister Ismene and fiancée Haemon (who happens to be Creon's son) she carries on with the repeated attempts to bury her brother, and, as the punishment she then is herself buried alive in a cave. When Creon changes his mind too late and breaks the entrance to the cave, Antigone is found already dead, having committed suicide, presumably choosing her agency again over a slow and painful death by starvation. As a direct result of her actions, her fiancée commits suicide too as does his mother.

When the facts of Sophocles' classic are put this way, it is very clear that the proposition that this is somehow the pinnacle of ethics one should aspire to is hardly attractive to a contemporary reader or spectator. And yet, Antigone, her dazzling beauty in her determination to do the thing she is committed to, has fascinated scholars, poets and writers for centuries. It is far beyond the scope of this essay to offer even the briefest of reviews of literature pertaining to this tragic figure over the centuries. Suffice to say that the play and Antigone herself has been a subject of speculations and re-writes by Racine, Hegel, Goethe and many others. She has been appropriated by the feminist icon and the radical thinker Judith Butler (2003). Most recently Bonnie Honig in her fascinating book *Antigone Interrupted* (2013) offers both a review of the scholarly work to date on Antigone as well as her own interpretations of what she might mean in the history of ideas and defiant stances against male authority. Honig's crucial move is to propose Antigone's act as interrupting a circle of trauma and chaos.

There are very many aspects to the Antigone tale and certainly one could offer a feminist critique demolishing Antigone's power and attractiveness as a role model. After all, here is a woman written by a man writer, who sacrifices herself for another man, her brother, at the hand of yet another man, for no great public cause and to no great effect. Horror and destruction follow. In the end, however, despite the unfashionable nature of somehow noticing the gender divide (the reluctance of course ironically being post Lacanian),[3] Antigone's 'no!' vis-à-vis Creon, a 'no' which she is willing to die for, and does – stands for the symbol of a young woman defiantly resisting the masculine narrative that masquerades as a display of power but is revealed as impotent as utterly unable to bring about any kind of resolution. Antigone's act is driven by her unconscious desire and love, according to Lacan, which then becomes a conscious decision. Her desire is to bury her brother but also it is a desire to find a closure to the trauma, and to the curse of her land and its people. As such, Lacan claims, anybody's ethical choice will resonate with that of Antigone: 'Even if you are not aware of it, the latent fundamental image of Antigone forms part of your morality' (Lacan 1992: 284). Let's see what Antigonian traits can be found in Maya.

If the events of 9/11 constitute an unspeakable trauma in which the body of the nation is irrecoverably wounded and altered, Maya's utter commitment to the project of finding and killing Bin Laden could be seen as a forced choice designed to restore some kind of equilibrium in her world. Like the action of Antigone, Maya seeks a final closure to the wars, violence and horror which preceded the sequence of events portrayed in the film. After an initial meek compliance, the quest to find Bin Laden becomes her life mission for which she believes she has been saved. Bigelow thus introduces a notion of destiny in the middle of this very contemporary and un-sentimental film. This is a move that does resonate with the notion of the Greek 'Atë' which I will return to later in this chapter.

As I am evoking Antigone and Lacan's reading of her in a discussion about a film about war, it is important to recall that it is in this seminar that Lacan questions the whole project of 'love thy neighbour' as something to aspire to. If you do anything noble, Lacan warns, there might well be, and usually are, other unconscious motives for your actions. It is perhaps just as well to be aware of them, rather than persevere with the idealistic and deceitful proposition of inner virtue.

Lacan sees a notion of polite goodness as unhelpful in defining what an ethical act is. He reminds us that Freud has a problem with the Love Thy Neighbour notion too and quotes from Freud's *Civilisation and its Discontents* (1930) saying that man's innate tendencies lead us to 'evil, aggression, destruction, and thus also to cruelty'. Man, he goes on to say, will use his neighbour 'to use him sexually without his consent, to appropriate his goods, to humiliate him, to inflict suffering on him, to torture and kill him' (Freud in Lacan [1959–60] 1992: 185).

There is thus a problem, which is both ontological, at the very heart of who we are as so called civilised people, and ethical. If we really follow our instincts, we might end up murdering each other more frequently than we do. But if we pretend to be good, this is hopeless too as leads to further deceptions and lasting corruptions of society through the very notion of charity. Controversially, Lacan criticises philanthropy, giving an example of St Martin as he gives his coat to a beggar. He claims that it is but a gesture which makes no attempt at understanding the heart of the matter here or meeting a real yearning on the part of the beggar:

> We are no doubt touching a primitive requirement in the need to be satisfied there, for the beggar is naked. But perhaps over and above that need to be clothed, he was begging for something else, namely, that Saint Martin either kill him or fuck him. In any encounter there's a big difference in meaning between the response of philanthropy and that of love.
>
> (ibid.: 186)

Lacan suspects any gesture of kindness is often tainted with other unconscious emotions, such as a need to control the Other rather than love him. Lacan comments sarcastically: 'It is a fact of experience that what I want is *the good* of others provided that it remains in the image of my own' (ibid.: 187, my emphasis).

In other words, as long as you are the Same and not the Other, I can be good to you. In contrast Lacan proposes a different approach to ethics: if you wilfully betray your readiness to keep discovering what your desire might be, or somehow submit to the demands of 'the service of goods', i.e. societal systems and procedures that destroy meaning, your very compromise is unethical. This is what Lacan goes on to say:

> And it is because we know better than those who went before how to recognize the nature of desire, which is at the heart of this experience, that a reconsideration of ethics is possible, that a form of ethical judgment is possible, of a kind that gives this question the force of a Last Judgment: Have you acted in conformity with the desire that is in you? [. . .] Opposed to this pole of desire is traditional ethics.
>
> (Lacan 1992: 314)

And a few pages later, he repeats again, positioning the psychoanalytic encounter in the same terms:

> I propose then that, from an analytical point of view, the only thing of which *one can be guilty is of having given ground relative to one's desire*. Whether it is admissible or not in a given ethics, that proposition expresses quite well something that we observe in our experience.
>
> (ibid.: 319, my emphasis, noting a different translation of the French as mentioned previously).

In order to be ethical then, one has to discover one's desire first of all and then be able to hold onto it, 'no matter what'.

Antigone and Maya

Lacan tells us at the outset that Antigone is beautiful, she 'is made for love rather than hate. In short, she is a really tender and charming little thing, if one is to believe the bidet-water commentary that is typical of the style used by those virtuous writers who write about her' (ibid.: 262). But quite quickly, according to Lacan, Sophocles lets us see Antigone's unfeminine strong mindedness, which frightens the Chorus: in her discussion with Ismene, her sister, she appears quite hostile and stubborn. Lacan points to the Chorus's disdain for Antigone: they cry out a Greek word 'ωμός' which Lacan says one might translate as 'infexible' (ibid.: 263).

But Lacan elaborates that the Greek word ωμός means more than just 'inflexible' namely:

> It literally means something uncivilized, something raw. And the word "raw" comes closest, when it refers to eaters of *raw flesh*. That's the Chorus's point of view. [. . .] This is then how the enigma of Antigone is presented to us: she is inhuman.
>
> (ibid.: 263, my emphasis)

There is therefore a connection between the body, 'the raw flesh', the destruction, and Antigone's desire. It is that determination, that 'inhuman' stubbornness performed unexpectedly by a beautiful young woman, which has disturbed the spectators' expectations both vis-à-vis Antigone and indeed Maya.

Maya as Antigone-like figure

Robert Burgoyne (2014) points out rightly that *Zero Dark Thirty* places the body at the centre of its articulation of history, amongst other elements, through Maya being forced to witness the enhanced interrogations carried out by her colleagues on the suspects right at the outset of the movie, following the harrowing audio recordings of those who perished during the horrors of 9/11. These enhanced interrogations were a response to the bodily trauma of 9/11 and the atrocities that followed. On her arrival Maya is immediately subjected to the trauma of witnessing a bodily abuse of the Other, and we as spectators are subjected to that trauma too. Clearly she got a job at the CIA voluntarily but we do know that when she first arrives at her new posting in Pakistan, it is not her choice ('did you want to come here?' she is asked and she answers – 'no!!'). Far from her being untouched by the tortures she witnesses (as suggested by Brown), Burgoyne points out that Maya's response is immediate, bodily and emotional. It is not that she is incapable of holding the gaze of the Other, it is that she is to start with too shocked by what she sees to want to look:

> Her hands at times covering her eyes, clutching her jacket, then forcing herself to watch, Maya is foregrounded in the scene's shot patterning: her experience of torture tracks an arc of emotion and performance that progresses from witnessing, to complicity, to coercive agency.
>
> (Burgoyne 2014: 5)

Burgoyne focuses also on a sequence in which Mayas studies on-screen footage of the endless interrogations in which she observes the torture with a view of learning something which might help the investigation. This is when she discovers the name Abu Ahmed – this is what is repeated over and over again. But in fact it seems that nothing else is discovered through this torture, and it is possible that that name was known before through more traditional intelligence as it is put forward to the prisoners. It is not that Bigelow condones torture. She shows us what the institutional procedures have allowed. The noises of disapproval on the parts of the critics vis-à-vis the director rather than the system which produced the procedures are to my mind misplaced. If anything, Bigelow is very careful to show that the actual effectiveness of the technique is at least questionable: the victims do not speak in a coherent way and the torturers, the nice well-educated American operatives, are so confused and traumatised by the experience that they appear to miss vital information even when it is given.

Brown rightly points to the importance of gaze in the film: the film's narrative is about that which is visible and that which is not. During the tortures demanding speech, the executioners demand that the prisoners look at them. *Zero Dark Thirty* like the play *Antigone* thus continuously links the gaze, the language and the body: these happen to stand for Lacan's three registers: the Imaginary, the Symbolic and the Real. It is as early as the seminar I am discussing here, given in 1957, Seminar VII (on Ethics), that Lacan clearly introduces the importance of all three[4] and certainly not just the language alone. We remember that Oedipus in an act of total impotence takes out his eyes as to vanquish his gaze: this he achieves but the Chorus and the spectators' gaze still torment him despite not seeing the horrors with his eyes. Bigelow makes us see the horrors. To blame her for insisting on the presence of the spectator's gaze is to confuse registers: she makes us look to confront our passive acceptance of the world we live in.

Maya's Atë

Lacan in his discussions of Antigone focuses on the word used in the Sophocles's original namely Atë – which can be translated as 'fate', 'destiny', and 'human misery'.[5] Lacan interprets Atë as a narrow range within which to operate and within this range it is important to find out what one's desire is and then to follow it to the end. Not everybody must make such a dramatic choice: 'One does or does not approach Atë, and when one approaches it, it is because of something that is linked to a beginning and a chain of events' (ibid.: 264). Antigone's Atë is that she is the daughter of Jocasta and Oedipus, the parents who committed unwillingly murders and incest, and that both of her brothers took part in a war against each other and that they are now both dead. This she cannot undo. But she can decide what to do faced with Creon's unreasonable edict.

What is then Maya's Atë and her destiny in *Zero Dark Thirty*? We know nothing about her background at all, apart that she joined the CIA very young. One could suggest that she shares her Atë with the rest of us post 9/11 – and particularly with those who were born in the United States: a long shadow of that tragedy that has cast darkness over contemporary history ever since. The film reminds the viewer what the world we live in now entails: wars all over the world in the name of peace, secret areas in which people are tortured in our name, unexpected terrorist attacks and countless deaths.

Maya's initial conversations with the female friend reveal that she has nothing in her life but work. She has no boyfriend, no lover, no friends, no hobby. This is what William Brown sees as a further proof of her 'war autism', her lack of empathy. Indeed even at the outset perhaps Maya already begins to appear a little 'inhuman', a little 'inflexible' like Antigone.

In Sophocles's *Antigone*, or rather perhaps Lacan's reading of it, there is a moment when she first of all laments her dead brother and her fate ('atë') weeping 'like a bird', simply a hurt young woman bemoaning her bad fortune. The moment of metamorphosis into the unmovable 'monstrous' comes after it becomes clear that Creon will not shift his position – Antigone's forced choice is a response to the immovability of the male ruler and his procedures as Shaviro would say. When it comes to it, the forced choice is a simple one: to give in or to continue to the end. In *Zero Dark Thirty* the key moment comes when Jessica, Maya's friend and colleague, also devoted to her work but perhaps in a more ordinary human way, gets blown up by a (male) suicide bomber.

It is the moment in which Maya, staring at the blank computer screen, is waiting for a reply which never comes, that marks her turning. It is an absence of either body or the language or indeed the gaze that makes her then more than inflexible: in her pursuit of her goal – she becomes 'monstrous', like Antigone. Maya does not lay her life for her cause, meaning she does not die in the film, but she has no life outside her mission. There is also no doubt at all that she would have given her life in a literal sense if that was what had been called for. We do witness her car being shot at – she carries on, to the end.

Maya's agency perhaps lacks the glamour of Antigone's undertaking as it mostly consists of her attempts to subvert procedural apathy of the patriarchal organisation she works for. To this end she is behaves

Figure 1.1 Maya (Jessica Chastain) in *Zero Dark Thirty,* staring at a blank computer
screen waiting for a reply

(Kathryn Bigelow 2012)

completely outside the accepted norms of institutional conduct, threatening and even abusing her exclusively male bosses and demanding she is given a freer reign. A female colleague draws her attention to the vital piece of information but when violence is actually carried out, it is always conducted by men in Bigelow's film. Once Maya's dogged determination succeeds and the order is given to instigate the attack on Bin Laden's den, she again is alone with a group of military men to whom she says: 'you will kill Bin Laden for me'. Her apparent bodily fragility and beauty, like that of Antigone, is in Bigelow's film juxtaposed with the physical roughness and strength of the men who are also somehow confused and uncertain as to what they are doing and why, despite having that procedural power still vested in them. The contrast between the (masculine) physical strength and the (feminine) mental strength and intellectual ability is striking in the film.

Before moving to the final section of this chapter, it is perhaps worth mentioning that the Lacanian call of not giving up on one's desire can create moral difficulties, which Žižek theorised as a possibility of being ethical but immoral at the same time (see Figure 1.2: Žižek's organisation

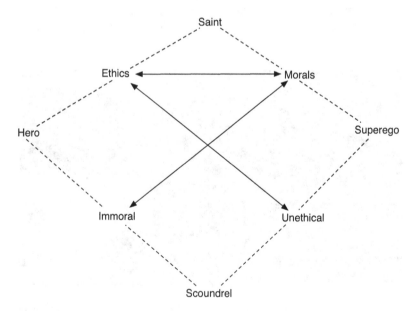

Figure 1.2 Žižek's organisation of ethics and morality into a semiotic square
(Žižek 2005: 67)

of ethics and morality into a semiotic square). I have cited and discussed this conundrum elsewhere (Piotrowska 2012: 14) in connection with the documentary film project.

Žižek says that

> [T]he saint is ethical (he does not compromise his desire) and moral (he considers the Good of others) whereas the scoundrel is immoral (he violates moral norms) and unethical (what he is after is not desire but pleasures and profits, so he lacks any firm principles).
>
> (ibid.: 67)

It is here that one could wonder again whether Maya's conduct and that indeed of Antigone was moral as well as ethical, given that their monstrous 'inflexibility' does cost innocent lives (in Antigone's case: the fiancée, the sister, her future mother in law etc.).

It is really Alain Badiou in his *Ethics: an Essay on the Understanding of Evil* (2002 [1993]) who presents a different approach, which by his own account draws from Lacan's dictum but is clearer and more exigent. He is very insistent that 'there can be no ethics in general, but only an ethic of singular truths, and thus an ethic relative to a particular situation' (Badiou 2002: lvi), although he did accept that one has to take into account the network of relationships it sustains. Badiou develops a list of criteria which define an 'event', a moment of revelation for the 'I' when a decision to act is taken. One of these criteria is a universal possibility of joining 'the event' which would differentiate it from a possible 'simulacrum'. So it was St Paul who decided to be the orator for Christianity after his revelation on the road to Damascus – and anybody else could have had this revelation. One could argue that both Maya and Antigone could fulfil Badiou's criterion: there are no a priori exclusions in either of their decisions. Badiou's ethic is a helpful and clear development of Lacanian ethics but its further discussion is beyond the scope of this chapter.

The beauty versus the horror

But there is something else going on here, both in *Antigone* and in *Zero Dark Thirty*. It is the main protagonist's gender, her youth and, most importantly, her beauty: the monstrous is also beautiful which confuses and fascinates the cinema spectator in the 21st century as well as *Antigone*'s Chorus and no doubt Ancient Greece's audiences. Lacan is very

careful not to invest Antigone's commitment to her cause with any libidinal undertones, which would have been such an easy move because of
her origins. But other scholars have wondered about it. Critchley (2007)
in his discussion of Lacan's notion of sublimation in Seminar VII makes
two points: the first one is in relation to one's (sexual) desire which
instead of being repressed is sublimated – somehow given an expression
other than a sexual one. The second point is to do with beauty, which is
inherent in sublimation of desire – at least in Seminar VII:

> What is the moral goal of psychoanalysis? 'the moral goal of psy-
> choanalysis consists in putting the subject in relation to its uncon-
> scious desire.' This is why the sublimation is so important, for it is
> the realisation of such desire.
>
> (Critchley 2007: 73)

In Seminar VII the person who sublimates her trauma through an act,
which is both beautiful and ethical, is Antigone. In *Zero Dark Thirty*
Maya's energies are sublimated into her project too with no space for
anything else. There is no physical sexual love in the lives of either
of these protagonists. Instead, they engage with the bodily ugliness
and horror of the war waged by men. Susan L. Carruthers (2013) in
her *Cineaste* article makes an observation that there is the 'Old Testa-
ment zeal' in Maya's work (ibid.: 52). But then, without referencing
any theory or psychoanalysis, she makes a point that there is something
'latently sexual about Maya's relentless quest for her man' (ibid.: 52).
And when the final moment comes after the hectic heist Carruthers again
connects to this to Maya's supposed latent sexuality: 'When she tilts her
head back, tears trickling, after the body bag's climactic unzipping, the
scene is suggestively postcoital: lips apart, hair tangled, chest heaving.
All passion spent' (ibid.: 52).

The preceding is not how I responded to the scene but the point is that
Maya's energy, perhaps her libidinal energy is present in the film and
sublimated into her mission. The scene of Maya identifying the body is
anticlimactic but meaningful. It is a scene in which Bigelow manipulates
the gaze through withholding the sight of the body. In the construction
of the film that gaze is not ours to hold: it is Maya's.

Robert Burgoyne sees Maya's beauty as disturbing 'the usual opera-
tive models' in the genre. For me it also resonates with Honig's notion
of a creative interruption. An 'interruption' might carry with it more
readily also positive meanings – that of a rupture which disturbs and

interrupts the status quo thus bringing about generative effects not least because of subverting the expectations of gender, class, race – and procedures. Its openness as named by Burgoyne (as follows), which I see as precisely such an opportunity. I cite Burgoyne's lengthy quotation on *Zero Dark Thirty* because it could also be applied to *Antigone*, both the play and the character, whose impact on thinkers, writers and our attitude to violence, commitment and ethics has been so immense over the centuries, and so very difficult to quantify. It is this disturbing and interrupting quality of the work and of the female characters, that Burgoyne comments on here:

> The character's youth and sculpted beauty troubles the paradigm of purposive violence; her striking 'whiteness,' for example, creates a disturbing and dramatic contrast of skin tones and textures during the interrogation scenes, producing a visual overtone, an Eisensteinian conflict, that is not easily accommodated by genre codes. At the same time, her beauty challenges the easy notion that violence is deforming and dehumanizing. Instead, the effect of violence on both character and history is left open, unresolved in the film's narrative program.
>
> (Burgoyne 2014: 251)[6]

Finally there is also the issue of Maya's face, at the very end of the film: a face for me not expressing any 'passion spent' after a sexual encounter but rather a realisation that her success might offer a closure of a kind but has carried with it death and further mourning too. This is reminiscent of Béla Balázs's writings about the importance of the close ups in feature film:

> The soul of a landscape or indeed any milieu presents itself differently at different points on its surface. In human beings, too, the eyes are more expressive than the neck or shoulders, and a close up of the eyes irradiates more sound than the entire body in long shot. The director's task is to discover the eyes of a landscape. Only in close ups of these details will he grasp the soul of its totality: its mood.
>
> (Balázs 2010 [1923]: 44)

It is Maya's final close up, reflective, tired, tearful but defiant, which defines what this film is about: an act which is tragic but ethical.

Final remarks

My point in this article has been that Maya's commitment to her cause is not engendered by her alleged lack of empathy but rather her conscious and stubborn commitment, however problematic and controversial it might be, to her chosen path. That commitment could be theorised as her 'not giving up on her desire' in Lacanian terms, thus constituting an ethical act. Maya's desire is fuelled by conscious and unconscious mechanisms, which the film hints at but does not spell out. What a Lacanian psychoanalytical reading can bring into a discussion of this film and others is a reminder of the unknowingness that is also a part of the human condition.[7] There is a lack of reasonableness about Maya which disturbs and interrupts viewers' accepted norms, particularly male viewers, and from that standpoint alone one could argue that it comes down in a line descending from Antigone, another inflexible stubborn and beautiful woman rejecting the rules and procedures of the patriarchal systems of her time in ways which some might view as immoral.

My very final thought is that it is a mistake to confine psychoanalysis to the particular structuralist readings of it which influenced the film theory post-1968 and which privileged language and identification. Psychoanalysis has always put body as a crucial focus of its interrogations. What Lacan reminds us of is that the Real, the body, and our desires, conscious or otherwise, come from complicated mixture of places, including our heritage, our place in history and society but also our ability to respond to our 'äte'.

Zero Dark Thirty is a decisive gesture, 'gesture' being a term describing film that Jennifer Barker deploys in *The Tactile Eye* (2009: 78). Despite its universal quality, what the film gestures to me is different to what it has gestured to William Brown or Susan Carruthers, for example, for a number of reasons, but certainly because we bring into the reading of it not only our scholarly experience, and the experience of watching films, but also our conscious and unconscious knowledge of the world, which includes our bodily position in it, including gender. It is not necessarily identification (Metz 1982) or empathy (Barker) that the film might evoke but rather our transferential relationship to its body, or 'its narrative program' as Burgoyne previously suggests, through our bodily response and our unconscious, which will contribute to it.

I am now turning my attention to a more classic re-formulation of a *femme fatale* in *Gone Girl* and *The Girl on the Train* in which a response to patriarchal violence is violence of a more basic kind.

Notes

1 For an excellent discussion of these procedures in the film please see Steven Shaviro's blog www.shaviro.com/Blog/?p=1114#comments) (accessed May 2016).
2 It appears that Lacan doesn't actually use this kind of invective but instead says: 'La seule chose dont on puisse être coupable, c'est d'avoir cédé sur son désir' [the only thing you can be guilty of is to have given up on your desire – my translation]. See Lacan (1986: 329).
3 Judith Butler's idea of gender's performativity in *Gender Trouble* (1990) has its origin in Seminar XX in which Lacan proposes that gender is not biologically determined.
4 Lacan's interest in the body grows until in Seminar XX it is his key focus of interrogation (a fact completely ignored during the heyday of post-1968 psychoanalytically influenced film theory and today).
5 Atë can be also translated as a delusion which leads to a disaster – this note was kindly given to me by Professor Richard Seaford, Professor of Classic and Ancient History at the University of Exeter in our discussions on Antigone.
6 See Richard Dyer (1997) for an insightful analysis of how 'whiteness' functions as a complex sign in film.
7 It is perhaps coincidental, and again unfashionable to point out, but the majority of the critics appalled by the film and Maya and cited by Greenwald in his piece mentioned previously are all male: Andrew Sullivan, Adam Sewer, Jay Rosen, Michael Tomasky, not to mention Slavoj Žižek who somehow has a blind spot for this Antigone-like figure, Lacanian though he is. I also choose to ignore here the very unfortunate use of the notion of rape as both a metaphor and comparison by Brown and Žižek in the works cited.

Bibliography

Badiou, A. (2002 [1993]) *Ethics: An essay on the understanding of evil*. Translated by P. Hallward. London: Verso.

Balázs, B. (2010 [1924]) *Early film theory: Visible man and the spirit of film*. Edited by E. Carter. New York: Berghahn Books.

Barker, J. (2009) *The tactile eye: Touch and the cinematic experience*. Berkeley: University of California Press.

Baron-Cohen, S. (2011) *Zero degrees of empathy*. London: Penguin.

Brown, W. (2013) 'War autism and film style: *Zero Dark Thirty*': https://wjrcbrown. wordpress.com/2013/11/12/war-autism-and-film-style-zero-dark-thirty/ (accessed 30 May 2018).

Burgoyne, R. (2014) 'The violated body: Affective experience and somatic intensity in *Zero Dark Thirty*', in LaRocca, D. (ed.), *The philosophy of war films*. Lexington: University of Kentucky Press, pp. 247–260.

Butler, J. (1990) *Gender trouble: Feminism and the subversion of identity*. London and New York: Routledge.

Butler, J. (2003) *Antigone's claim: Kinship between life and death*. New York: Columbia University Press.

Carruthers, S. L. (2013) *'Zero Dark Thirty'* [review], *Cineaste* 38 (2), pp. 50–52.

Collins, K.A. (2018) 'Reexamining the "Zero Dark Thirty" backlash cycle, five years later', *The Ringer.com*: www.theringer.com/movies/2018/2/26/17055154/zero-dark-thirty-backlash-kathyrn-bigelow-2013-oscars (accessed 4 June 2018).

Critchley, S. (2007) *Infinitely demanding: Ethics of commitment, politics of resistance*. London and New York: Verso.

Dyer, R. (1997) *White: Essays on race and culture*. London and New York: Routledge.

Freud, S. (1930) 'Civilisation and its discontents', in *The standard edition of the complete psychological works of Sigmund Freud, Volume XXI (1927–1931)*. Translated by J. Strachey. London: Hogarth Press and the Institute of Psychoanalysis, pp. 86–145.

Greenwald, G. (2012) 'Zero Dark Thirty: CIA hagiography, pernicious propaganda', *The Guardian*: www.theguardian.com/commentisfree/2012/dec/14/zero-dark-thirty-cia-propaganda (accessed April 2018).

Honig, B. (2013) *Antigone interrupted*. Cambridge: Cambridge University Press.

Keysers, C. (2011) *The emphatic brain*. Munich: Social Brain Press.

Lacan, J. (1986 [1959–60]) *Le séminaire. Livre VII: l'éthique de la psychanalyse*. Paris: Seuil.

Lacan, J. (1992 [1959–60]) *Seminar VII: The ethics of psychoanalysis 1959–1960*. Translated by D. Potter. London: Taylor and Francis, Routledge.

Lévinas, E. (1981) *Otherwise than being*. Translated by A. Lingis. The Hague: Martinus Nijhoff Publishers.

Piotrowska, A. (2012) 'The conman and I: A case study in transference in documentary', *Studies in Documentary Film* 6 (1), pp. 15–29.

Wolf, N. (2013) 'A letter to Kathryn Bigelow on Zero Dark Thirty's apology for torture', *The Guardian*: www.theguardian.com/commentisfree/2013/jan/04/letter-kathryn-bigelow-zero-dark-thirty (accessed 4 June 2018).

Žižek, S. (1989) *The sublime object of ideology*. London: Verso.

Žižek, S. (2005 [1994]) *The metastases of enjoyment: Six essays on woman and causality*. New York: Verso.

Žižek, S. (2013) 'Zero Dark Thirty: Hollywood's gift to American power', *The Guardian*, 25 January: www.theguardian.com/commentisfree/2013/jan/25/zero-dark-thirty-normalises-torture-unjustifiable (accessed April 2018).

Zupančič, A. (2000) *Ethics of the real: Kant and Lacan*. London: Verso.

2   The killjoy and the nasty woman in *Gone Girl* and *The Girl on the Train*

It would be good if it were possible to begin this chapter by evoking a sense of walking into a multiscreen installation with many ideas and images presenting themselves at the same time. The diagram I have created (see Figure 2.1) represents some of the ideas that have fuelled this chapter.

The key notion to bear in mind (and that features in the diagram across all the fields) is that one could argue that cinema as a whole is a metaphor – a metaphor for our contemporary concerns and preoccupations. How then we analyse the cinema in ways that at least get close to this complexity is a problem. If the issue is that language itself and academic writing in particular is still the domain of patriarchal thinking,

Psychoanalysis	Fantasy	Feminism
Ethics	Violence	Desire
Anger	Love	Embodiment
misogyny	fear	scholarship
metaphor	metaphor	metaphor
Violence	Desire	Love
Race	Binaries	Death
Racism	Nomadic	Time
ideas	Post-human	Technology
metaphor	**metaphor**	**metaphor**

Figure 2.1 Diagram evoking the different ideas and emotions present in this chapter

then it would be wonderful to get rid of its restrictive rules altogether and start again. This of course is a time-honoured desire by women writers of the 20th century, arguably led by the French *l'ecriture feminine*, which was a good example of such an attempt.[1] Hélène Cixous (1976) describes *l'ecriture feminine* through a variety of metaphors, including milk, orgasm, honey and the ocean; she claims that *l'ecriture feminine* serves as a disruptive and deconstructive force, shaking the security and stability of the phallogocentric Symbolic Order, and therefore allowing more play – in gender, writing and sexuality – for all language-using subjects. This could include personal reflection alongside academic thinking, for example.

Feminist scholar and writer Sara Ahmed, whom I mention later in the chapter, tries and re-tries another way of disposing of the white man's language, as she calls it, through writing more freely to the point of deciding against quoting any white men, or in any event those who are involved in the building of the Western canon of thinking. The latter constraint – however tactically appropriate in her case – I question as a practical person: I will take whatever I find on my travels, including good ideas by white men. This chapter lends itself to experimenting with different ideas and manifold textures of expression, as this conversation is about multiple ways of seeing women's place and power and creativity in the concrete case studies of the two – or rather three – films under discussion. It is about fantasy and the limits of what is acceptable in a given paradigm within that fantasy. What becomes clear very quickly is that these limits are different for different people, and a reading of these films constitutes a discussion about one's position in the world and is therefore important beyond the particular texts.

The chapter is about the nasty women in *Gone Girl* (2014) and *The Girl on the Train* (2016) against the backdrop of David Lynch's classic *Blue Velvet* (1986), which arguably sets a standard for an exploration of the dark side and the hidden beneath the pretty and the safe. This chapter offers a few reflections on fantasy and desire in cinema and its limits, and what constitutes a male fantasy we can live with and a female fantasy we love – or loathe. How do we as 21st-century gender-fluid viewers and multimedia users deal with the representation of violence and desire in cinema, the representation of roles that involve re-defining the notion of agency and perhaps masculinity vis-à-vis femininity? In times when the necessity of moving beyond simple binaries becomes clear and enunciated by many feminists (because the binaries don't seem to work and because they do not describe the world we live in adequately) what can a viewer learn from a film like *Gone Girl* beyond its violence, its game-like manipulations and the battles for power?

The word I have omitted in my opening diagram is 'suburbia', which in the three films functions as a metaphor as well as a concrete space. In some ways it denotes the safe, middle of the road, middle-class space that is out of the urban grittiness but also not quite the wild countryside. It is a metaphor for the lie of the suburban life that offers a tedious and ultimately unproductive and false haven but which in reality hides dark fantasies, secrets, deep frustrations and desires. This setting we know from a number of films located in Middle America (from *Back to the Future* (1985) to *The Tree of Life* (2011)) but perhaps none more than David Lynch's suburban classic *Blue Velvet*. *Blue Velvet* is an excellent counter point to *Gone Girl* and *The Girl on the Train* – both in terms of the metaphor of the hidden and the invisible in suburbia but also in terms of the cinematic text's relationship to the desire, fantasy and sexual violence it conjures up and puts on display.

In this chapter, I will also reflect on some ideas by Sara Ahmed from her recent book *Living a Feminist Life* (2017). In particular, her idea of the 'feminist killjoy' seems close to the 'nasty woman' notion: a feminist who disrupts stable situations and norms, if necessary at a high cost to herself – and to others. I will also take issue with the view presented by notable feminist psychoanalyst and scholar Jacqueline Rose who in her short article in the *London Review of Books* (2015) expresses her utter dismay at the two novels on which the films are based (*Gone Girl* and *The Girl on the Train*), calling them deeply misogynistic and unhelpful to the feminist cause.[2] Whilst Rose makes some excellent points, there is a different way of thinking about the representation of the 'perverse protest' in these films, a term coined by Lori Marso (2016: 870) in connection to Simone de Beauvoir defining marriage as 'perversion'. Marso's article points out similarities between *Gone Girl* and *Jeanne Dielman* (1975) – *the similarity being the violence that a woman commits against a man*. The latter is recognised as a feminist classic in stark contrast to *Gone Girl*. It might be the provenance of the works as well as the aesthetic choices made by the filmmakers, but it is good to bear in mind as we walk through different arguments. It is the notion of 'the perverse protest' which is significant in this discussion.

Importantly, there is also the tradition of the *femme fatale* that the books and the films are drawing from. It is the reversal of the role that the *femme fatale* can play in *film noir*, which I claim is worthy of reflection. Here the female protagonist is created not just as fodder of the male desire, for she is more than beautiful and sinister. She becomes an agent who pushes events forward on her own to the point of committing violence herself.

Ahmed's notions of the 'feminist killjoy' (Ahmed 2017: 23) and a wilfulness in carrying out a stance which is against the polite acceptance of the existing norms, might be useful in constructing an argument for the productive nastiness of the main characters of the films I am concerned with. I will also attempt to deploy Audre Lorde's ideas here (2017), however difficult a task this will be. Positioning these films against David Lynch's *Blue Velvet* made in 1986 is an exercise, which at a stroke, puts the question of agency at the heart of this conversation. What happens to the viewer's desire when the woman is no longer a passive object of fantasy – on the part of the filmmaker but on the part of the spectator, too? What happens when the subjectivity of the *femme fatale* is tested as she becomes a real nasty villain capable of a real nasty crime – within the constraints of the fantasy space that is cinema? Where does it leave us, the spectators, who are used, and yes, very used, to a different representation of female and male desire?

Misogynist?

In her *London Review of Books* feature of 2015 (2015: 25–26), Jacqueline Rose expresses her complete and utter disgust and horror at the novels (*Gone Girl* and *Girl on the Train* written by Gillian Flynn and Paula Hawkins respectively). She states that she would not bother to see the films as apparently they are 'even worse' (ibid.: 25). She sees the two novels as an unwelcome re-presentation of 'hatred of women' (ibid.: 25). For Rose the work reifies violence, presenting women as the unstable carrier of it in society:

> One of the reasons for the success of *Gone Girl* and *The Girl on the Train* may be that they make violence not just compelling, like any horror story, nor just manageable, like detective stories (which always reassure us that the worst will finally be contained by the law), but digestible, a bit like consuming a TV dinner, legs outstretched, in an armchair. Sitting there (metaphorically), I felt I was being invited to identify as a reader with a man – a man not

particularly sexual, or fit or even menacing, in fact someone who is pretty bored by the world – for whom misogyny just happens to be the best show in town, and, since both these stories were written by women, simply a fact of life that has nothing to do with him (even if, as we will see, he just might be a killer).

(ibid.: 26)

Rose goes on to say that in these novels 'hatred of women is a nonchalant kind of pleasure' (ibid.: 26). As the novels are written by women, one has to wonder whether Rose sees them as a kind of patriarchy imbued self-hatred, in which women reproduce the patriarchal patterns of behaviour and thinking without challenging them. Clearly, my reading of the novels and the films is different.

There is a point worth making here straight away: first, the two novels have little in common except for the 'girl' in the title and the first-person narrative. Why they are often put together might be because of the proximity of the dates of publication of the novels and the production of the films as well its thriller-like genre.

Nonetheless, there are some similarities. One key feature in the construction of their narratives in both the novels and the films is a similar stylistic device, insofar as the structure is polyvocal, that is, both novels use the device of different first-person narrators presenting their story. Mikhail Bakhtin, an important literary theorist, discussed this kind of polyphonic inter-textuality as adding an extra depth to a novel's plot and narrative as well as to character building.[3] Through seeing the world from different points of view, interwoven in one novel, the viewer has a chance to be a co-creator of the work: the different perspectives offer a dialogue. In *Gone Girl* there are two voices, Amy's and her husband Nick's: Amy herself has two voices – her fake diary voice, created to fool the police and to frame Nick, and her more truthful internal voice.

In terms of the narrative, *Gone Girl* offers the movement of the narrator who is also the main character (Amy) from a 'nice girl', in fact a super nice girl, to a super nasty woman. *The Girl on the Train* presents a contrary movement to *Gone Girl*. By the time we meet Rachel, and indeed the others, nobody is 'nice' at any point any more. The movement, however, is from a nasty if useless woman to somebody who travels through a journey of a concrete discovery, which makes her find herself again. There are different voices of women but the key one, that of Rachel, is confused and muddled since the main character is an alcoholic who has forgotten who she is, has lost her husband, her home and a job, and her mind too – or so it seems to begin with.

The constructions of the character are different: in *Gone Girl* the writer creates an unreliable narrator who is unreliable very deliberately and whose very assertion of who she is therefore in the end becomes problematic. The writing is clearer and to my mind more powerful than that of *Girl on the Train* and the purpose is very clear too: to create a persona in the first part of the book through a diary which is a lie in order to deceive the reader/viewer so that the revelations as to the actual events come as a big surprise. One could venture, taking the Lacanian dictum that 'truth has a structure of fiction' (Lacan 2006: 684) that the fake diary in a way is not just a lie, as the narrator does tell us key things about her existence and the meeting of her husband Nick, whom she loves desperately and for whom she agrees to mould herself into the 'cool girl', one of Flynn's sharpest observations of contemporary life and contemporary gender relationships. While I will come back to the notion of the 'cool girl' later in this chapter, it is important to note that Nick, far from being the supportive new man she imagines him to be, undermines her life and the persona she has created for herself. This is another similarity between the two novels – the female characters end up feeling rage against their men, and that rage arguably leads to the corruption of their agency. They either become confused, drunk, lost and then violent (Rachel) or they become menacing, cruel and horrifically violent in the fantasy of regaining their lost identity and power (Amy).

In the second part of *Gone Girl* this is not a diary anymore written by Amy, the main character, for the police to find; it is what we are to believe her actual thoughts and feelings. Nick Dunne's narrative in the novel is mostly of a selfish and ordinary man's account of expecting quite extraordinary sacrifices from his girlfriend and then wife, without giving it much thought. In return, he cannot be supportive to her at all, he cannot love her, he betrays her sexually and in every way that one human being can betray another – for he takes away from Amy who she is and replaces it with vacuous lies. So far so familiar. The surprise comes when the narrative takes an unexpected turn. What Flynn does brilliantly, and Paula Hawkins too, using different tools, is subvert the predictable narrative. The fantasy of the idyll of suburbia and the perfect togetherness, which in the first instance appears to be a domestic melodrama story of the woman silently suffering as a victim, takes a different turn. However abhorrent Amy's actions are, however psychopathic her character becomes, she gains and asserts full agency.

This is Flynn's construction of the 'truth' of the events as they unfold, including the deceptions of the main character, the creation of the person she is or pretends to be. When Nick first meets her she is a beautiful, incredibly clever, successful and wealthy New Yorker in her early 30s. Once 'settled' down and married, she has to give up her way of life, her independence and New York in order to be a perfect wife or at least in order to create a marriage as perfect as it was possible to create under the circumstances. However unreliable this narrator is, some elements are repeated in the second account: if we are to believe anything of the novel and the storytelling, we must believe that Amy did try to change for Nick. She did try very hard to become the impossible 'cool girl' for him and it is he who betrayed her and that project. Her violence comes out of her sense of profound betrayal by her husband. The representation of how her agency became corrupted is therefore emphatically not misogynistic. It is instead a bold and risky re-imagining of what female desire and agency might be, and what rage, fuelled by male violence and betrayal, might actually look like. It is a metaphor, not a self-help manual.

Jacqueline Rose instead sees something different: '*Gone Girl* is the perfect enactment of a brand of misogyny that has women's minds – as much as, or more than, their bodies – in its sights' (ibid. 26). Rose's proposition is that both novels – and films – are misogynist in a way that is insidiously buying into a patriarchal system of thinking about women, that they are dangerous if not controlled, that their intelligence such as it is demonstrated is to be deployed as a deranged and destructive power. This is what Rose goes on to say: 'In fact, the two books are mirror images of each other. If in *The Girl on the Train* women lack intelligence, in *Gone Girl* the woman has too much, which she uses to torture her husband with the cruellest precision and effectiveness (in a corresponding symmetry, this means that men are either killers or puppets on a string). Either way, intelligence is not something women deploy to any good' (Rose 2015: 26).

These are dramatic statements which one can take issue with. The conflation between the films and the books goes on and I go on with it here up to a point; it is not a totally mistaken course of action to take, for the films are fairly faithful renditions of the novels, *Gone Girl* more so than *Girl on the Train* (which moves the whole action from the UK to the States). The attitude towards violence in the films is important. David Fincher's adaptation of *Gone Girl* makes the film significantly more violent than the book. Tate Taylor's *Girl on a Train* does exactly the opposite: the very violence at the end of the *Girl on the Train* novel, which Rose objects to, is not only softened in the film but simply eradicated: Rachel and Anna do not murder the main villain of the film. They overpower him and call the police. They are able to use the system to their advantage. There is also a mere suggestion of a possibility of an alliance between the two women who have been rivals throughout – a new element in the film and the genre of neo-noir. It is also significant that violence is avoided despite the man in question being the actual murderer. They control him together but they do not kill him.

Gone Girl's treatment of violence in the film is pointedly different from the book. While violence simmers just under the surface throughout the novel, Fincher's film makes it explicit. As a director, Fincher is not known to revel in on-screen violence – even in a film such as *Fight Club*, the title of which seems to suggest that violence is a necessary element of it, violence is often more metaphoric than actual. In *Gone Girl* he concretises it.

On the opening page of Gillian Flynn's *Gone Girl*, Nick Dunne introduces his wife Amy with a graphically detailed description of her brain:

> When I think of my wife, I always think of her head. [. . .]
> I'd know her head anywhere.
> And what's inside it. I think of that too: her mind. Her brain, all those coils, and her thoughts shuttling through those coils like fast, frantic centipedes. Like a child, I picture opening her skull, unspooling her brain and sifting through it, trying to catch and pin down her thoughts. *What are you thinking, Amy?* The question I've asked most often during our marriage, if not out loud, if not to the person who could answer. I suppose these questions stormcloud over every marriage: *What are you thinking? How are you feeling?*
>
> (2013: 3; emphasis in the original)

In the film the opening section is very similar but significantly different, much briefer and much more concretely violent:

> When I think of my wife, I always think of her head. [. . .] *I have pictures of cracking her lovely skull, and spooling her brains, trying to get answers*. The primal questions of any marriage. What are you

thinking? How are you feeling? *Who are you? What have we done to each other?*

(my emphasis – this is about 2 minutes into the film)

Ben Affleck's voice is heard over the back of Rosamund Pike's head, blond hair filling the frame, with her head then moving towards the camera and her face looking so beautiful and innocent.

The final shot of the film is very similarly framed but the expression of the Amy's character's face is very different: the innocence is gone and instead a slightly sad, knowing look features. The illusion of any kind of harmony is gone: this battle for supremacy in the marriage has been fought – and won: by the woman.

The naming of the violence lurking in the original narrative is concretised here which has the effect of naming what the film in part is about – the inherent violence of hidden fantasies in a subject's psyche.

The key violent scene of the film is the one where Amy kills her ex-boyfriend, whom she is staying with in order to hide from everybody who is looking for her. In the novel, Flynn sets up the situation in which her apparently hapless and deeply devoted friend is slowly but surely bullying her, depriving her of any sense of freedom, forcing her to lose weight again and dye her hair blond in order to comply with his wishful thinking and his desired image of an idealised woman. Of course, such a typically male form of control is no excuse for her killing him. In the book the actual description of the murder is economical. Flynn focuses more on Amy's mental processes of deciding that this will be the only

Figure 2.2 Amy Dunne (Rosamund Pike) in the opening scene of *Gone Girl* (David Fincher 2014)

way forward but also including a low-grade cruelty by her host: it is clear what her life would have been like had she decided to stay. In the book therefore her choice is not as simple as in the film: the violence that follows might possibly be the only way forward or out, given the circumstances she put herself in. It is in this context that Flynn creates the scene where Amy once again falls in love with the image of her husband declaring on television that he loved her and that he was sorry. Despite knowing full well that he is lying, she chooses the suburban fantasy over being a prisoner of a controlling man she despises. In the film the murder is shockingly violent, not so in the novel.

I shall resist the temptation of suggesting that a male director's treatment of the story added the violence and the misogynist elements to it. It is unclear why Fincher did this. Particularly the horror-like murder scene, with Amy covered in blood, feels like it belongs to a different genre. I offer this observation simply as an observation – the film is more violent than the book and it makes *Gone Girl* appear more misogynistic. It is possible that the filmmaker wanted the suggestive violence to be more concrete for the dramatic impact of the film, for example. Nonetheless, it is very clear that there would have been many ways of directing that scene, making it less horrific. David Fincher makes sure the spectator will not easily forget this image.

This is perhaps a good moment to return to David Lynch's portrayal of suburbia. *Blue Velvet* is a classic *neo-noir* film in which sex and violence are interwoven very closely, in ways often uncomfortable for the viewer who is put in the position of a voyeur of violent scenes – although arguably not as violent as those in *Gone Girl*. The film has been written about extensively. It has attracted a substantial body of criticism by feminist scholars, particularly those engaged with psychoanalysis. Whilst, as mentioned, some did question the film's representation of women, a surprising number defended the film. I will briefly review here some of the voices critiquing the film at the time.

Barbara Creed (1988) acknowledges the film's provenance as a typical *neo-noir* and advances the argument that the film constitutes a 'send-up of Freudian themes'. She claims the film is parodic and should be read as a '*hysterical* text' (1988: 97; emphasis in the original). She proceeds to point out that the important aspect of fantasy for Freud was not its relationship to reality, but its degree of psychical reality in the life of the individual. She reminds us that:

> According to Laplanche and Pontalis, whose article 'Fantasy and the origins of sexuality' has been a key point of reference in this

debate, [Freud] saw psychical reality as 'alone truly real, in contrast with the majority of psychological phenomena'; it is just as 'real' as the material world.

(Creed 1988: 98, quoting Laplanche and Pontalis (1968)

Creed explores the film from the classic psychoanalytical point of view of a child's primal fantasies and the organisation of the sexual field of a child, quoting John Fletcher who claims that early development assigns the gender positions constructed for life: 'masculine/active, feminine/passive' (ibid.: 98)

Creed emphasises the voyeuristic elements of the film, with young Jeffrey secretly witnessing the violent sexual encounter between Dorothy and perversely violent Frank who appears to evoke a sense of confused sadomasochistic desire, in which we as viewers partake as we observe Jeffrey observing the scene. Creed – as well as Laura Mulvey (1996), Lynne Layton (1994), and others – emphasises the rather obvious re-formulation of the Oedipal plot in which Jeffrey has to kill the father figure and his own perverse desire for the beautiful but dangerous mother figure (Dorothy) in order to be able to become a man and develop a wholesome union with Sandy (played by Laura Dern).

In connection with this fantasy unfolding, Creed reminds us that, according to Laplanche, the position of the spectator in relation to this primal scene fantasy is aligned with masochism. He compares the infant to Tantalus, who was forced to watch the spectacle of his parents engaged in the act of copulation. Its passive position, claims Laplanche, 'is not simply a passivity in relation to adult activity, but passivity in relation to adult fantasy intruding within him' (Laplanche, quoted in Creed 1988: 109). Creed adds: 'Thus Jeffrey's voyeurism is counterbalanced by this passivity and helplessness' (109). Viewers too re-discover this early childhood trauma of witnessing a sexual encounter between one's parents (109).

Creed points out that our position as the spectator is that of a voyeur drawing pleasure from suffering:

Frank's brutalization and conquest of Dorothy are a taming of woman and the terror she holds within herself. [. . .] Dorothy is partly presented as the phallic mother because of her placing in the desires of the male protagonists. These desires are spoken through a staging of the three primal fantasies, and they shape the structure of the narrative. But desire for the son is also Dorothy's desire. In this sense she holds the key to male pleasure and happiness and she knows it. This is why Frank screams at her not to look at him. *He cannot bear to see that she ultimately holds the power.*

(ibid.: 113; my emphasis)

Laura Mulvey (1996) also focuses on the Oedipal aspects of the film and its fetishistic fixations, but making and additional point about the film's links to the Gothic novel and even to horror films. She applies Vladimir Propp's *Morphology of the Folk Tale* (1968) to identify narratives and patterns, pointing out Lynch's iconography which conflates the underworld of the criminal, the netherworld of the city at night, with the unconscious of the Oedipal drama (Mulvey 1996: 142). She, too, places the spectator as a voyeur enjoying this unfolding of the Oedipal coming of age story, be it in dark and uncomfortable circumstances. Mulvey also reminds us of Raymond Bellour's gloss of the Oedipal scenario:

> The bad father must die, in the final confrontation, so that the couple can be formed; he even has his double, his reverse image, the good father, who makes possible the entry into the genealogy, the continuity between generations. . . . It is the movement from the adventurer, *sans foi ni loi* as we say in French (lawless and faithless) to the husband, the future father and the good citizen. . . . The American cinema thus finds itself enacting the most classic paradigms elaborated for the subject of Western culture by Freudian psychoanalysis. . . . My constant surprise was to discover to what degree everything was organised according to a classic Oedipal scenario which inscribed the subject, the hero of the film, in a precise relation to parricide and incest and to observe that his itinerary, his trajectory corresponded to a strict psychic progression which engaged the hero in the symbolic paths of Oedipus and of castration.
>
> (Bellour, quoted in Mulvey 1996: 143)

Layton too offers a further discussion of the Oedipal complex in the film wondering whether Dorothy is fundamentally powerful as the holder of the male desire (of both Frank and Jeffrey but also other men in the bar in which she performs. She is clearly an impersonation of the fatal beauty everybody dreams of subjugating.)

As I re-read these articles in 2018 after all the revelations of the #MeToo campaign and the Harvey Weinstein scandal, I feel a number of overwhelming emotions, which I will attempt to unpack and share here. First of all, the whole Oedipal story, which forms the mainstay of

Freud's theory and which clearly is re-presented yet again in *Blue Velvet*, feels anachronistic and deeply patriarchal in a way which renders it (the theory and the film) simply irrelevant. I have not quoted these Oedipal readings of the film for any other reason but to make the following point: what is important and disquieting are the feminist scholarly attempts to present Dorothy as somehow powerful despite the fact that she is repeatedly abused. It is quite extraordinary that both Barbara Creed and Lynne Layton (Laura Mulvey at least pulls back from the assertion) interpret Dorothy as in the end holding all the power. She is raped and beaten but somehow the writers still say she holds the power. To my mind the fantasy in *Blue Velvet* appears to be exactly the opposite: the powerful phallic mother is overwhelmed and eventually castrated by the usual domestication of the *femme fatale*: she is seen at the end of the film as safe, but devoid of her mysterious attractiveness, simply a single mother with a little son. If there was a protest in her perverse conduct then the viewer never has a chance to see that rebellion – simply because it is not there. Her delivery from evil is accomplished by the very same person who also accidentally abused her (Jeffrey). To frame her deranged seduction of the young man as anything other than a repetition of the abuse she has just suffered appears a deeply ingrained patriarchal reading of the violence and the fantasy in the film.[4]

Blue Velvet is a brilliantly made surrealist-inspired disturbing film about what might lie beneath clean white houses, but the fantasy and desire it represents is male and male alone and the female characters in it are totally devoid of agency. They are subjected to violence but incapable of defending themselves in any way. The Isabella Rossellini character, as the beautiful and mysterious Dorothy, is completely humiliated and subjugated before she is 'saved'. She is literally seen stripped of any dignity and agency, naked and wounded in the streets, begging young Jeffrey for help, in front of the somewhat shocked Sandy, who realises that her newly beloved might have fantasies and desires she does not know about and possibly will never be able to fulfil. Rather curiously, anticipating the fantasy of the 'cool girl' already referred to, Sandy agrees to be all things for her man, of course. However exciting and innovative *Blue Velvet* is, it is in the end a portrayal of an Oedipal coming of age in which the woman is but a fodder for the development of this fantasy.

Furthermore, re-reading the learnt articles by the renowned psychoanalytically influenced female feminist scholars who have written thousands of words analysing, re-interpreting and somehow validating this fantasy in which the woman is but the object of man's desire and fantasy, I became angry in an un-scholarly way. It is indeed illuminating to think through why writers such as Sara Ahmed suggest that we should stop reading white male thinkers. Does this studying of the patriarchal thought not lead to this perhaps unconscious nauseating repetition and legitimising of the patriarchal point of view? However much I admire David Lynch as a film-maker, I have no interest whatever in seeing Isabella Rossellini raped and humiliated on screen in yet another re-telling of the Oedipal myth.

To put it bluntly therefore, I argue that *Gone Girl* and *The Girl on the Train* attempt to grab hold of the kind of rage that I have just felt and imagine it as an actual concrete violence – against men, against their violence and against the patriarchal way of thinking which still seeps through everything we do.

The representation of such a fantasy is still only possible through female characters who have deep psychological issues. Amy is an ultra-intelligent but damaged child prodigy turned psychopath and Rachel is an alcoholic who has lost herself completely due to the abuse, violence and deception of her husband. Far from being misogynistic these texts offer a re-imagining of the suburbia story in which a woman like Dorothy fights back. Sadly, this fantasy/metaphor of 'fighting back' offers no new ideas of how to re-negotiate the balance of power in the world.

It is interesting to consider briefly how *Gone Girl* might fit into the construction of the classic psychoanalytically influenced feminist film theory which in essence proclaims that cinema reinforces masculine identity at the expense of feminine identity. Mulvey famously appropriated psychoanalysis 'as a political weapon, demonstrating the way the unconscious of patriarchal society has structured film form' (Mulvey 1975: 6). In terms of image, cinematic techniques (elements of *mise en scène* such as camera movement, framing, editing) turn the woman into a fetish object (via the male gaze) exactly as it does in *Blue Velvet*:

> The woman as icon [is] displayed for the gaze and enjoyment of men, the active controllers of the look. [. . .] fetishistic scopophilia builds up the physical beauty of the object, transforming it into something satisfying in itself. [. . .] Fetishistic scopophilia [. . .] can exist outside linear time as the erotic instinct is focused on the look alone.
>
> (ibid.: 16)

Mulvey reminds us that most classical films (that would include *Blue Velvet*) follow the Oedipal narrative structure. Films typically end with the 'formation of the heterosexual couple', while female characters who do not conform to patriarchy are punished (the *femme fatale* in *film noir*; Judy in *Vertigo* (1958), etc.). Second wave feminist film theory analyses both the patriarchal construction of woman as image and also focuses on her narrative function, her place in the patriarchal plot. In *Gone Girl*, as in *Vertigo* and *Marnie* (1963), the process of (female) image construction becomes part of the story. Amy's parents, for instance, create a series of books based on Amy's life, called *Amazing Amy* – and the character in part needs to establish a viable relationship to the image of her which the world expects. As Nick says: 'Your parents literally plagiarised your childhood', to which Amy replies: 'No they improved on it'. However, as previously stated in the construction of this character, even in her final decision, she takes control over her image – along with her desire. Amy, in her role as a *neo femme fatale* and in contrast to other *femmes fatale*s is not punished for transgressing the symbolic role assigned to her. She appears to be domesticated but viewers know that this is but a façade, a re-positioning of the game in which the image turns out to be the most important element. Nick appears passive and pleasant but actually he is but a fairly lazy man, ready to sacrifice anything for any form of gratification. As a character, he is the post-Oedipal heir to Jeffrey from *Blue Velvet*, but the narrative of both book and film does not let him off the hook as easily as it does in *Blue Velvet*. He is exposed, he is called out as an ineffectual, scared, morally flawed individual who perhaps deserves what befalls him.

It is here that it is worth mentioning briefly Lori Marso's (2016) sophisticated reading of a number of films featuring violence committed by women, including *Gone Girl*. She offers a reading of the films through the lens of Simone de Beauvoir's classic *The Second Sex* ([1949] 2011). Marso points out that some of the violence in *Gone Girl* could be interpreted as a 'perverse protest' (the term coined by de Beauvoir) and she goes on to say: 'With Beauvoir, we can see how women's seemingly pathological feelings and acts of violence, produced in isolation and conditions of oppression, might be read as signs of resistance' (2016: 870).

In order to look for ideas of 'feminist collectivity and solidarity', I turn to voices in feminism outside the established white canon.

Lost desire and the killjoy?

How do we deal with the violence that men have perpetrated against women for centuries and the rage that this violence evokes in a woman – and when I say 'we' I do mean women in the first instance, any women in any culture but also mean 'we' the spectators, the multi-gendered hybrid spectators who watch the films presented to them and who may choose to treat them as metaphors and symptoms for the times we live in. How do we keep looking for different alliances, without giving in to the rage and without giving in to the patriarchal system?

Sara Ahmed begins *Living a Feminist Life* (2017) with the following provocative statement: 'Feminism is sensational. Something is sensational when it provokes excitement and interest. Feminism is sensational in this sense; what is provocative about feminism is what makes feminism a set of arguments that is hard to deliver. We learn about the feminist cause by the bother feminism causes; by how feminism comes up in public culture as a site of disturbance' (2017: 21). The book itself is sensational in a way an academic book can be – not 'going viral' sensational like a YouTube video or an incriminating tweet, but Ahmed has unleashed a Twitter storm and enlivened blogs. Nor can an academic book compete with either of the two films under discussion, whose audiences count in tens of millions. *Living a Feminist Life* nonetheless has ambitions to reach a large number of women, opening modes of thought about what it means to be a feminist in different ways; very uncomfortable ways on many occasions.[5]

Ahmed's central idea is that of a 'feminist killjoy', tactically deployed as a weapon of resistance vis-à-vis patriarchal power and combating the notion of 'a nice woman' who, culturally, we are all interpellated to be from birth. Ahmed instead advocates a 'willful' (2017: 15) adoption of resistance to the inclination of being compliant and making people 'happy'. This wilful attitude, by definition, is in direct contrast to the notion of the 'cool girl' as presented by Gillian Flynn in *Gone Girl*. The feminist killjoy is nasty by definition. In order to create ruptures to patriarchal ways of thinking, she will be deliberately stubborn on certain issues and this stance will involve upsetting people, disrupting accepted ways of communicating, being perceived as rude even. In short, without actually using the term, Ahmed does suggest that the only way forward in the world is to be a 'nasty woman'. What Ahmed calls 'willfullness' is not only a resolve close to stubbornness that tolerates no compromise, but a preparedness to live with the consequences of one's actions – beyond reasonable limits, and with no regard to the price to be paid in personal happiness or isolation from the community. In this respect, the willfullness of Ahmed's killjoy is not dissimilar from Lacan's Antigone: a woman prepared to see through her conviction to the death, no matter what (a stance which I discussed at length in the introduction and in Chapter 1 of this book on *Zero Dark Thirty*).

In *Blue Velvet* there is another female character who is juxtaposed to the character of Dorothy and who is discussed less readily: this is the young Sandy (played by the beautiful and the very young Laura Dern) who is indeed the original 'cool girl', the definition coined by Amy in *Gone Girl*, of a (young) woman who is game for anything, and who is prepared to be everything that a man wants her to be without putting any demands on him at all. She is good looking, charming, thin, well educated, has a good job, gives blowjobs, is innocent but adventurous and also endlessly supportive and forgiving. She is an impossible patriarchal fantasy pretending to be a post-feminist success. The 'cool girl' harps back to the perfect housewife in Chantal Akerman's film *Jeanne Dielman* who performs all the mundane womanly tasks perfectly until one day she kills a man.

In *Gone Girl* the cool girl's reward as sarcastically described by Flynn is that she gets the man – as long as she pretends not to have any conditions or demands, including emotional ones. Sandy in *Blue Velvet* is indeed such a cool girl: she supports young Jeffrey in his detective pursuit without asking many questions, she offers him vital information without really understanding why he might need it, she gets involved in his schemes simply because he asked her to, and is ready to forgive when she realises he fucked the beautiful but deranged Dorothy. She is ready to be the perfect response to the male desire – yet again!

The ending of the film shows the two in the happy idyll of the suburban life – the danger has passed and the suburban can carry on. This is where one could venture *Gone Girl* and to some extent *The Girl on the Train* begin – perhaps indeed as a 'perverse protest'.

Could one then say then the cinema of *Gone Girl* and *Girl on the Train* and the nasty woman in these films goes some way towards opening a space in the mainstream cinema which in some way builds on the experimental work of Chantal Akerman, without of course being aware of it? Its violence offers a space in which non-Oedipal kinds of metaphors, fantasies and desires might yet take place. It is a project under construction but hope remains.

Final nomadic thoughts

I come back to a sense of wanting an installation of many screens, which would at least signal the many ideas that run through this chapter. Braidotti and Haraway's ideas of inclusivity and building new allegiances need repeating here, for the continuous re-inscription of the binaries is self-limiting.

First, of all, I have a sense I ought to explain why I still use psycho-analysis in my thinking and writing when its foundational idea is the Oedipal myth, the repetition of which I find nauseating. Unknowing-ness of the Other, developed further by many feminist thinkers, includ-ing Judith Butler, who works with it in her book on getting close to the other (2005). I have based a lot of my academic work on the oeuvre of Jacques Lacan in part precisely because the Oedipal story is not the main focus of Lacan's topology. Quite the opposite: in his later work, particularly Seminar XX (1999), Lacan makes a crucial point that gender is not biologically determined which in its turn indeed has influenced the ground-breaking earlier work of Judith Butler (1990) and others. The issue is not with the biological gender of the thinker; the issue is whether the thinking opens new spaces. The issue with the Oedpial myth as the foundational story of psychoanalysis is precisely the problem named previously – it deals with male desire and male subjectivity alone. Frankly, it is not just conservative and patriarchal, it is simply tedious and not very generative. Not only does it not allow for female desire or fantasy independent of male desire, it allows for no other forms of masculinity. Worse still, it does not allow for it being even imagined. I, and many others, use psychoanalysis without giving the supremacy to the endless re-telling of the Oedipal myth.[6]

On this final stretch I would like to turn to different thinkers for inspi-ration, for new ideas and thoughts. The films under discussion present a white middle class nasty woman-cum-femme fatale who is either subju-gated in a violent way (*Blue Velvet*) or becomes furiously violent herself. In this short monograph the strategy I have adopted is to look at very particular film texts situated in Western culture. There reason for it has been multifold but it is also fair to say that 'the nasty woman' and the *femme fatale* is not a ubiquitous figure in film world cinema although she does begin to rise and I hope to interrogate her in a separate project.

Why then do I bring into the conversation black feminists when the cinema under discussion is certainly not black? It is certainly not any kind of tokenism but rather the recognition of the importance of the ideas that white feminists too can learn from. So what can we learn from black feminist ideas, which perhaps can be used to begin to think of dif-ferent allegiances?

There are a number of issues with Sara Ahmed's stance and presenta-tion, her charismatic strong voice notwithstanding. For me, the key issue is her interpretation of intersectionality as being close to excluding the experience of white women and all men as well as conflating various black female voice into one in the conversation about feminism. It is clear that a white woman has the white privilege that a black woman does not – this in itself is a sweeping statement that immediately needs challenging and justifying: the woman of colour on the whole struggles more than a white woman. Does a black woman struggle more than a brown one? Is the issue of exclusion really the main focus here? Stressing the difference without a solution is an issue. This has been indeed pointed out by Mariam Rahmani (2017) in her review of Ahmed's book. Taking a cue from Sarah Ahmed's call for non-patriarchal ways of expressing one's arguments, I offer here a brief auto-ethnographic account of my experience of being the Other.

As a Polish woman with a very Polish name living and working in the United Kingdom for 25 years, I feel aggrieved at being excluded from a conversation about levels of discrimination in this country and elsewhere. Nonetheless as I have asserted elsewhere (2017) I do appreciate and get the advantages I have by the sheer fact of my embodiment and of belonging to the Western cultural tradition. I question however the notion that discrimination or unconscious bias is to do with embodiment alone. The position in society, one's origins and the perceived and actual class is of key importance. Finally, I would like to add a personal anecdote which speaks to the notion of female solidarity across the cultures and embodiments.

In 2016 I was producing and co-directing an African film noir, *Escape,* in Zimbabwe which did involve a nasty woman indeed, a *femme fatale* played beautifully by a bold and talented Nothando Nobengula. On set there were a number of tensions and conflicts, I would say largely to do with me being a woman and directing a large team in which the production and technical teams consisted exclusively of men. The film was a collaborative process carried out through a partnership I set up in Zimbabwe with an acclaimed Zimbabwean filmmaker, Joe Njagu, a young man in a hurry who was my co-producer and co-director as well as the director of photography on the shoot. In hindsight, the public display of my power in these circumstances was something difficult for him to deal with and so he put himself quite separate from me during the shoot. I felt he did not support me. On the other hand, the large contingent of various women on the shoot, including the cast, stood by me like a wall of strength and solidarity. They did support me, against their male colleagues, their partners and boyfriends. The alliance was built across the race divide, and the embodiment divide and on this occasion it worked. To repeat: the black female members of the team supported me in solidarity against their African male colleagues. They supported me despite my whiteness and my privilege because I was a woman leading largely a male team and doing a good job, or a good enough job, in the face of grave difficulties presented by the men in the team. Their support was tangible, moving and unforgettable.

Finally, I would like to reference some thoughts by Audre Lorde, the extraordinary black feminist writer and thinker (whom Sara Ahmed references in her work), especially her notion that erotic energy needs to be a part of a discourse about power and progress.

The notion of an importance of touching is not a new one and I have written about it extensively elsewhere (Piotrowska 2017), referencing in particular the difficulties of performing a touch in the colonial context and quoting Nancy and Derrida in their affirmation of a touch constituting a moment which changes any circumstance and involves a movement. Feminist Luce Irigaray talks about the importance of touching and sexuality in communications and the encounter with the other (2008). Audre Lorde does something else and something more: she urges to use the erotic feminine agency to change the world, to change the way we can think and communicate and to undermine the white man's celebration of rational thinking. Lorde talks about 'the erotic as a considered source of power and information within our lives' (Lorde 2017: 22) and urges women to use it as a powerful tool against patriarchy. She despairs over women coming 'to distrust that power which rises from our deepest and non-rational knowledge' (ibid.: 22–23). She sees stripping of the ability to get in touch with our bodies and trust them as one of the reasons for the female subjugation over the ages, the Black woman in particular, but actually any woman: 'In touch with the erotic, I become less willing to accept powerlessness, or those other supplied states which are not native to me, such as resignation, despair, self-effacement, depression, self-denial' (ibid.; 28).

Lorde sees the erotic charge as an energy which is deeply feminine and brings forward strength which comes from a different place to a cool rational thinking but is as authentic and important and can lead to transformations if you allow yourself to trust it:

> Recognising the power of the erotic within our lives can give us the energy to pursue genuine change within our world, rather than merely settling for a shift of characters in the same weary drama. For not only do we touch our most profoundly creative source, but we do that which is female and self-affirming in the face of racist, patriarchal and anti erotic society.
>
> (Lorde 2017: 30)

This is a good place for me to stop a conversation about a killjoy here and begin a conversation about ways to transform the world through creative endeavours which re-define the space and through the transformative power of the erotic, which can be scary as well as generative but which, in the end, brings about light out of utter darkness. The next two chapters are about the nasty woman in Sarah Polley's documentary *Stories We Tell* and then Andrea Arnold's ground-breaking and unsettling film *Red Road*.

Notes

1 The following offers a good account of *L'ecriture feminine* and Hélène Cixous:

> Freud calls women 'the dark continent,' and Cixous uses that as a metaphor to celebrate the lack of control possible over the position of woman in the phallogocentric Symbolic Order. Feminine writing is associated with the Lacanian Real, with the maternal body, which is barred from the Symbolic Order; she associates representational writing with the Symbolic, and non-representational writing with the female and maternal bodies. Feminine writing does not belong exclusively to females, however; Cixous argues that anyone can occupy the marginalized position of 'woman' within the Symbolic, and write in l'ecriture feminine from that position.
>
> (Klages 2012)

The notion of using contradictions in one's writing and acknowledging bodily influences on the work, against strict notions of patriarchal scholarship, is made non-biological gender dependent.

2 Rose is but one amongst many voices criticising the films as non-feminist.

3 For a discussion of Bakhtin's concept of 'polyphonic inter-textuality' see Harder (2018).

4 It is worth mentioning in passing Žižek's discussion of *Blue Velvet* as a treatise on desire (2012) or Todd McGowan's more sophisticated discussion of the links between desire and fantasy in Lynch (2007).

5 Mariam Rahmani, for example (2017), acknowledges the book's power but questions Ahmed's ability or indeed willingness to listen to others and to share the experiences which would question her own stance.

6 In the collections I have edited or co-edited with Ben Tyrer (2015, 2016), that is *Embodied Encounters and The Unrepresentable*, one can see a whole variety of psychoanalytically deployed thought which is feminist and situated in the body.

Bibliography

Ahmed, S. (2017) *Living a feminist life*. Durham: Duke University Press.

Butler, J. (1990) *Gender trouble: Feminism and the subversion of identity*. London and New York: Routledge.

Butler, J. (2005) *Giving an account of oneself*. New York: Fordham University Press.

Cixous, H. (1976) 'The laugh of the Medusa', *Signs: Journal of Women in Culture and Society* 1 (4), pp. 875–893.

Creed, B. (1988) 'A journey through *Blue Velvet*: Film, fantasy and the female spectator', *New Formations* 6, pp. 97–117.

De Beauvoir, S. (2011 [1949]) *The second sex*. Translated by C. Borde and S. Malovany-Chevallier. New York: Vintage Books.

Harder, H. (2018) 'A few introductory remarks on Bakhtin and Intertextuality': www.scm.uni-halle.de/reporting_list/study_days/sektion1/2303855_2303900/ (accessed 28 April 2018).

Irigaray, L. (2008) *Sharing the world*. London: Continuum.

Klages, M. (2012) '*L'ecriture feminine*': http://bloomsburyliterarystudies.typepad.com/continuum-literary-studie/2012/03/lecriture-feminine.html (accessed 25 April 2018).

Lacan, J. (1999 [1975]) *Seminar XX: On feminine sexuality, the limits of love and knowledge*. Translated by B. Fink. London and New York: W. W. Norton.

Lacan, J. (2006 [2002, 1999, 1971, 1970, 1966]) *Écrits*. Translated by B. Fink. New York: Norton.

Laplanche, J., and Pontalis, J. B. (1968) 'Fantasy and the origins of sexuality', *The International Journal of Psychoanalysis* 49 (1), pp. 1–18.

Layton, L. (1994) '*Blue Velvet*: A parable of male development', *Screen* 35 (4), pp. 374–393.

Lorde, A. (2017) *Your silence will not protect you: Essays and poems*. London: Silver Press.

Marso, L. (2016) 'Perverse protests: Simone de Beauvoir on pleasure and danger, resistance, and female violence in film', *Signs: Journal of Women in Culture and Society* 41 (4), pp. 869–894.

McGowan, T. (2007) *The impossible David Lynch*. New York: Columbia University Press.

Mulvey, L. (1996) 'Netherworlds and the unconscious: Oedipus and *Blue Velvet*', in *Fetishism and Curiosity*. London: BFI, pp. 137–154.

Mulvey, L. (2009 [1975]) *Visual and other Pleasures*. London and New York: Palgrave Macmillan.

Piotrowska, A. (ed.) (2015) *Embodied encounters: New approaches to psychoanalysis and cinema*. New York: Routledge.

Piotrowska, A. (2017) *Black and white: Cinema, politics and the arts in Zimbabwe*. New York: Routledge.

Piotrowska, A., and Tyrer, B. (eds.) (2016) *Psychoanalysis and the unrepresentable*. New York: Routledge.

Propp, V. (1968) *Morphology of the folktale*, second edition. Translated by L. Scott. Austin: University of Texas Press.

Rahmani, M. (2017) 'Facing the Feminist in the mirror: On Sara Ahmed's "Living a feminist life"', *Los Angeles Review of Books*: https://lareviewofbooks.org/article/facing-the-feminist-in-the-mirror-on-sara-ahmeds-living-a-feminist-life/ (accessed 22 June 2018).

Rose, J. (2015) 'Corkscrew in the neck', *London Review of Books*: www.lrb.co.uk/v37/n17/jacqueline-rose/corkscrew-in-the-neck (accessed 23 June 2018).

Žižek, S. (2012) 'On David Lynch', *Lacan.com*: www.lacan.com/thesymptom/page_id=1955

3 The nasty woman as a deceiver and a creator in Sarah Polley's *Stories We Tell*

Preliminary remarks

There are two pretty nasty women in *Stories We Tell* (2012) – the mother and the daughter. This is a pretty bold statement and I will qualify it directly but the fact is both the mother and the daughter in the film are certainly not very nice, at least within the framework of patriarchal and conservative thinking: the mother appears to have been pretty promiscuous all her life, resulting in abandoning of her first family and children and then in being unfaithful yet again in her second marriage to the point of getting pregnant by another man, without ever sorting out her personal circumstances, thus deceiving her husband, her daughter and the whole family as to the provenance of her child. It is perhaps too much to call Diana a neo *femme fatale* but some of the *femme fatalish* elements are in place in her character for sure: she is pretty, she uses men to her own advantage, she uses her sexuality – and sadly, like a classic *femme fatale*, she dies, exiting the patriarchal stage, not strong enough to carry out the fight – like in many *noir* movies.

The daughter is the filmmaker, Sarah Polley. She is pretty nasty too. She carries out her project of making the film with a single mindedness worthy of the Lacanian hero and his reading of Antigone: with a total commitment to her desire (the making of the film), with little or no consideration for her family, who are made to perform revealing her utmost private feelings for her ruthless camera in the spectacle of her creation. She puts them on display for reasons that are never totally clear, not even to the filmmaker herself. This nasty woman betrays the most basic rules of decency, love and respect, including her mother's desire to keep things secret, her father's peace of mind, and her family's kinship structures. She disturbs it all, ruthlessly and violently, in making her film. She also destroys some things irrevocably, and perhaps in particular her

(non-biological) father's sense of self-respect and identity and his trea-
sured belief that she, Sarah, was a longed for lovechild by him and his
late wife Diana, a child who was the fruit of the unexpected and late
revival of the passions between him and his wife. Instead, Polley reveals
that all this was but a façade erected by the other nasty woman in the
film, her mother, in order to hold onto her comfortable life.

In addition to all of this, this nasty woman in the guise of the filmmaker is very nasty to us all: to the viewers. She lies to us. She deceives
us. She pretends that she uses family archive throughout the film but in
fact she does nothing of the sort. Instead, she mixes the real home movies with the dramatic reconstructions she herself made up. She does it
without telling us about her scheme. In fact, the extent of her deception
is never quite established. We do not know which material is true and
which is this fake archive. By doing this she evacuates her own sense of
confusion and betrayal onto the viewer. One could argue that her gesture
is deeply unethical and that the result is but a suspect investigation into
her family's pain. Why on earth would anybody do such a thing and
why on earth would I devote the whole chapter to this unethical project?
Clearly, these are provocative statements that I do not hold completely
true. Nonetheless, it is important to acknowledge the stakes here: viewers are the victims of the nasty woman filmmaker. But in truth, is she
really that nasty? Or does she choose to deal with her personal childhood
trauma in a creative, empowering and radical way?

Figure 3.1 'Archival fake footage' in *Stories We Tell*
(Sarah Polley 2012)

Everybody has a troubled childhood. Psychoanalysis sets up its stall by maintaining that we all carry in us an originary trauma. Colette Soler stresses that Freud highlights the repetitive return of childhood suffering, real and imaginary in transference in all clinical encounters (Soler 2015: 12). Some of us can 'do' something with this pain through sublimation (which I will come back to in due course) – something artistic or scholarly, that redirects the hurt into a new kind of creation. In the spirit of subverting a straightforward patriarchal scholarship, I shall offer some personal reflection here before moving onto the detail discussion – and a defence – of the nastiness of Sarah Polley. My own childhood was indeed haunted by whispers and secrets. In addition, the systemic lies exacerbated by the validation of lying as a legitimate mode of conduct by the then totalitarian system in Communist Poland made even the simplest of lives difficult: there was pain, deceit and trauma at the core of the political system that nobody was allowed to spell out clearly: the most surreal circumstances occurred daily – an announcer on the news would claim a record production of meat, for example, and yet there was only vinegar and green peas in tins in the shops.

This disjunction between facts and fake news was felt deeply a long time before anybody would dream of the current crises of credibility in contemporary political systems. The sense was that everybody lies – on television and within your family too. My memories of these early days feature my own curious suspicions regarding the provenance of my arriving in the world. I discovered much later that almost every child worries about who they might really be and if they really belong to the family they find themselves in. But there were indeed real secrets in my family. I also remember looking through early black and white photos of my early childhood, searching for proof that this indeed was my birth family, even then thinking of technology as bringing forward the final proof of truth.

Later still I learnt that my mother was 'the other woman' in somebody's marriage, that my parents wondered whether they should abort me and that somewhere in the world there is a woman who thinks she is my biological half-sister. I have never met her and I will never meet her as this was the express wish of my late father and his first wife: that woman must never know she was adopted and they were concerned I would not be able to keep the secret. I sometimes have an overwhelming desire to look for her and pretend we are in fact actual sisters even though we have never met.

As a filmmaker, all my life, one way or another, I have been writing about love and the difficulty of experiencing it. I have made curious documentaries (*Married to the Eiffel Tower* (2008) to name one) and now am beginning to make fiction films about attachments that have been just too all-consuming to be good for us. I have however stayed away from documenting any actual personal trauma of my own life and putting it into public domain.

Sarah Polley's *Stories We Tell* addresses a personal childhood trauma head on. As such, it is a bold, controversial and inspirational documentary. I suggest that the film offers a reparative space for the filmmaker and perhaps, ultimately, for her viewers, too, through its use of obsolete technology, or rather through the filmmaker's choice of using a simulacrum of the technology in question: a pretend Super 8 film that never was. In this chapter I draw on Foucault's work (2013) on ethics to argue that the use of technology in *Stories We Tell* enables the filmmaker to create a space of reparation for herself and a space for self-care, self-reflection and vigilance for the participants in the film. The film consists of the filmmaker carrying out interviews with the members of her close family in order to ascertain what really happened in her childhood, what kind of person her mother might have been behind the appearances of a happy and fulfilled person and, finally, who the filmmaker's biological father was. Early on Polley introduces a home movie family archive, announcing that her father filmed it after her parents' wedding. Polley then proceeds to use the supposed archive footage throughout the documentary to support her narrative. She never reveals that some of it is fake. I argue that on the filmmaker's part this can be read as a gesture of defiance against the patriarchal structures of production of knowledge as well as a filmmaking technique enabling her exploration of her own past. In this chapter I will discuss the ethics of such a gesture vis-à-vis the filmmaker's family too.

The question of the ethics of a documentary text has been debated for decades (cf. Cooper 2006; Cowie 2011; Lebow 2008; Renov 2004; Rothman 1998; Winston 2001). My own contribution to this debate (Piotrowska 2014, 2015) focuses on the relationship between the filmmaker and the subject of her/his film and how that 'secret' relationship might influence the way in which the film is perceived by the spectator, without the latter fully realising what might have gone into that relationship. I used psychoanalytical paradigms to frame this process (calling it 'the documentary encounter'), focusing in particular on the parties' unconscious desires, which might well be different from their stated objectives. In this context, I introduced the psychoanalytical concept of 'transference' (2014: 6–13), a deeply fantasmatic attachment that takes place in the clinical session between the analyst and the analysand in order for the work to be able to take place at all. 'Transference' can produce a feeling similar to love, thus clouding the judgment of those involved in the process – be it in the clinic or outside it. Freud was aware of this mechanism already in 1915 (Freud 1958 [1915]) and urged his trainees not to act on it (i.e., not to engage in sexual relationships with the patients, but just to use the mechanism for therapeutic work). He also knew that 'transference' took place outside the clinic, as did Lacan, who evoked the notion of the 'subject supposed to know' (*sujet supposé savoir*), present in all his writings and developed in detail in Seminar XI (1998 [1981]), where the attachment is aided by an asymmetrical power relationship. I have argued that transference takes place in the 'documentary encounter' too, particularly when intimate or traumatic matters are discussed over a period of time (2014: 30–45).

Due to unconscious but powerful narcissistic desires of wanting to see a more beautiful reflection of oneself (thus replicating the mirror stage) or in somebody's gaze (as theorised by Donald Winnicott), the encounter between the filmmaker and her subjects is always, I claim, close to an unethical gesture, particularly from the point of view of what Levinas proposed as the 'Infinite Responsibility for the Other' (1961: 171). The special bond between filmmaker and subject is inevitably broken when the former involves a third party – a broadcaster, a viewing public, an editor even. Using Lacan's paradigm of the three registers, I suggest that the process of making the work public marks a shift from the Imaginary to the Symbolic, a movement Lacan called suture. It is this shift that in a documentary film can amount to an unethical gesture and a sense of betrayal on the part of the participant in the documentary because, in essence, what was given in love, is now utilised for a public spectacle. The documentary encounter becomes even more complex when the filmmaker is a member of the family, as is the case with Polley's *Stories We Tell*. It is clear that the relationships in the encounter are fuelled by 'transference' to facilitate the process at all. A sense of deceit and hurt is palpable in the participants' interviews and their moments of silence that Polley chooses to keep in the film.

Childhood trauma

Stories We Tell addresses notions of lack, loss, mourning and melancholia in a direct and material way: the mother of the filmmaker is dead and the film is a way of dealing with that loss – but it is also a search for some kind of truth and perhaps reconciliation. I suggest that through the 'secret' recreation of false archive images of her childhood without acknowledging their fakery, the filmmaker both takes charge of the past and also offers herself and her family the possibility of a different future: if her mother, exercising her freedom, ended up only making futile gestures against the patriarchal system, then, conversely, Sarah Polley takes charge of proceedings more resolutely – perhaps also transferring her own sense of being betrayed (by her mother) onto the viewer by 'betraying' them in turn with fake footage. My main argument in this chapter is that Polley re-positions her trauma through a new technological language via film footage of events that may or may not have taken place, while simultaneously *omitting* to tell us, the viewers, about her decision – perhaps to deal with her trauma more creatively. There are multiple ethical issues to address in this situation: if there is a possibility of a special bond developing when people work together in discussion of deeply personal issues – as is the case in the clinic and, as I claim, also in some circumstances outside it – then creating an encounter within close family circles, which interrogates those deeply felt issues again for the purposes of turning it into a public spectacle, might be deeply problematic.

Before proceeding to look at the film, I want to mention some additional psychoanalytical notions that might be helpful in the analysis of the ethical aspects of *Stories We Tell*. One of these is the Freudian notion of afterwardness, *Nachträglichkeit*, introduced in the context of a suppressed trauma which becomes significant only in due course, and not at the time of the experience. Lacan reformulates this Freudian notion in his work as *après coup* (deferred action), which he sees as a key clinical concept. With *après coup* Lacan suggests that language can re-organise the past through changing the chain of signifiers of the traumatic memory (or non-memory); it thus offers a possibility of changing the future too – one can also think about it differently, namely that a possibility of imagining a different future, will change the past, too. In *Stories We Tell*, this change of signifiers (the filmmaker's creation of the fake archive footage) functions as a kind of prosthesis for the filmmaker, which she uses to re-gain power that has been lost by her mother – attaining the agency, perhaps, her mother never really had.

Film, performance, performativity and reparation

In recent scholarship on film and the body, Davina Quinlivan has introduced the notion of 'reparation' through the film experience. In her discussion of *Waltz with Bashir* (Folman 2008) in particular, she poses a question about the spectator and his or her relationship to the film as 'a reparative object' and situates it in modes of recuperation in the 21st century (Quinlivan 2014: 103). Quinlivan is concerned with the possibilities of 'the film's healing "body" for the spectator' (ibid.: 104). To this end Quinlivan discusses Vivian Sobchack's and Laura U. Marks's haptic film theories before examining the generative possibilities of Melanie Klein's work on reparation.

I would like to take up the notion of reparation in film too, but suggest that in *Stories We Tell* the reparative work only takes place on the side of the filmmaker, which offers, at best, a space for *reflection* rather than reparation for the spectator. The space in which the documentary filmmaker creates her work with the Other (in this instance, the filmed subjects) is still a contested space, as it may be too difficult to interrogate in a scholarly way, for the filmmaker-filmed subject relationships are often hidden and secretive. However, in *Stories We Tell* at least some of Polley's tools are on display: they are presented in a tangible form within the documentary. The space is therefore possible to analyse – at least partially.

At the outset, the filmmaker exposes the construction of the film, thus appearing to make it a kind of performative documentary, a mode Bill Nichols defines as paradoxical because 'it generates a distinct tension between performance and document, between the personal and the typical, the embodied and disembodied [. . .]. These films stress their own tone and expressive qualities while also retaining a referential claim to the historical' (1994: 97–98). In other words, performative documentaries are not slavishly tied to a referent or to what 'really happened' (ibid.: 99), for they also reference memories and impressions, conveyed not factually but affectively. This is evident in the title of Polley's film: a documentary with the title *Stories We Tell* is not limited to the description or explanation of historical facts, but focuses on the process of storytelling from someone's particular perspective. Such films 'invoke an epistemology of the moment, of memory and place, more than of history and epoch' (ibid.: 105), and embody a defamiliarising effect (ibid., 99). It is worth recalling that this kind of defamilarising or distancing effect (*Verfremdungseffekt*) was considered by both Bertold Brecht and the formalists as a form of empowerment for the viewer, since it deconstructs, to a certain extent, the process of the making of the work, theatre in Brecht's case or indeed cinema (see Oever 2010), thus enabling the viewer to be more than a mere passive spectator – the viewer sees how the film or a theatre play is made and therefore becomes a co-author of its reception. I also argue elsewhere (Piotrowska 2014: 83) that not editing yourself (the director) out of a documentary film is in itself an ethical gesture, giving the viewer a chance to question the production of knowledge in the text.

Since Nichols, additional scholarship has emerged on the nature of the performative documentary (Bruzzi 2000; Lebow 2008). In *First Person Jewish* (2008), Alisa Lebow makes an interesting observation about the creation of her film *Treyf* (1998) and also her own reaction to the work once she became a spectator. First, she unashamedly confesses that the film's characters were *similar* to who they were, but they were also clearly made up:

> We, the filmmakers of *Treyf, invented* our characters Cynthia and Alisa, based, like many compelling representations, on true stories. [. . .] *Truth demands a story, for it cannot be told otherwise*, and in the telling it is always altered – truth being, then, alter to itself. So too, Alisa and Cynthia, the onscreen characters, are other to ourselves, no more or less true than any other story we tell about ourselves.
>
> (Lebow 2008: 89; my emphasis)

This observation echoes Lacan's contention that truth has a fictional structure (Lacan 2006: 684). Lebow says that the whole film was billed as 'semiautobiographical' (2008: 99) – 'semi' in order to signify a degree of 'creative licence' the women used in their self-representation. With hindsight, she regrets that word 'semi' – the work was fictionalised, but it was true.

Michael Renov (2004) has discussed subjectivity in autobiographical texts, while Brian Winston (in a conference paper of 2017)[1] has challenged the easy assumption that comes with the term 'performative documentary'. I would add that the performative has the potential to confer upon the historical and the social 'a sense of the local, specific, and embodied' (Nichols 1994: 106). This balance between the impersonal (history, society) and the personal (individual memory, affect) makes the performative an ethical mode of documentary filmmaking, involving not only the filmmaker's willingness to disclose her/his tools of the craft, the levels of honesty and courage but also, perhaps, her/his philosophical, or at least cultural stance in the world.

In *Stories We Tell* the performance by the filmmaker, and, by extension, the performativeness of the piece of work as a whole, is thus an artifact that escapes easy assumptions and categorisations. Psychoanalytical framing assists in understanding what might be going on here but does not offer a full explanation. The filmmaker indeed introduces herself and her father at the outset as the key characters of the whole film, and hence seems to evoke the *Verfremdungseffekt* mentioned previously as well as the filmmaker's/the film's performativeness: he is seen with her in a studio getting ready to record his commentary. Straight away, he asks her questions about the real motives of her project. By placing him at the heart of the film as the person who actually narrates it, Polley makes him a peace offering and a kind of an apology for subsequently dismantling his world and for making his shame (after all he is the cuckooed husband who brings up somebody else's child) a spectacle for us to see.

We later learn too that her biological father, a famous film producer in Canada and the man her mother had an affair with, demanded that the story is his to tell, which Polley refused in a determined way, taking the whole creative power firmly in her own hands. This we do learn, but some things are never revealed to the viewer at all; the initial 'performative' gesture is therefore in the end not entirely empowering for the viewer who is deceived by the fake archive footage – the footage which pretends to be the family Super 8 but is in fact the filmmaker's creation.

The gesture thus appears but a performance of a kind instead of being performative. To put it bluntly, it is a lie the filmmaker offers to the viewer – which means it is not a Brechtian *Vermfremdungseffekt* after all and appears deeply unethical. Instead, the filmmaker's position is that of an 'unreliable narrator'; the continuous mediation between trust, truth and emotion is the key element of the film, with its use of technology being a crucial player. This mediation is assisted and facilitated by the controversial use of the fake archive – which is not really disclosed as such until the end – and even then, it is extremely brief and could easily be missed on first viewing: we realise that much of the film was a performance only when we see the long credits of various actors playing the filmmaker's family members. Let's pause here briefly to consider the use of this technology in the film.

Obsolete technology, sublimation and sinthome

In an unpublished lecture on the 'poetics and politics of obsolescence' arising from digital technologies, Thomas Elsaesser draws attention to the fact that in *Stories We Tell* the obsolete technology, in the guise of the Super 8 camera, has a particular role to play in the re-writing and re-telling of Sarah Polley's traumas. It would not have been the same to somehow offer a re-enactment of her past without the image matching the original image produced with the now obsolete technology. As Elsaesser says:

> I was struck by the way this Super 8 camera, in its precariousness and obsolescence, became a talisman and fetish (in the anthropological sense) charged to document and to uncover what the actual surviving images so carefully hid and concealed, namely the mother's extra-marital affair, of which Sarah turns out to have been the not altogether welcome love-child. It is as if the re-staging and faking is actually Polley's 'working through' and 'acting out' of the trauma of her paternity, for which the Super 8 camera itself as object becomes both the instrument of truth, and the guarantor of authenticity, in the very act of filming the unfilmed, and thus restoring what is missing in Sarah's life narrative.
>
> (Elsaesser 2014: 5)

Viewers are never given enough material to understand the complex relationships between the people Polley introduces as her elder siblings, but who, we later discover, are actually her half siblings. As we begin to realise that many things are not what they seem, several questions are raised in the viewer's mind: did she know some of her brothers and sisters only as occasional strangers? Are they the children her mother left? Are they real people? Or maybe actors? Is there something wrong with the archive? What is this film doing to me? What was the timeline for all this? Why are we not told more? What's going on? Can we trust this filmmaker at all? One could suggest here also that the whole film is in a way a re-enactment of the confusion and pain the filmmaker herself must have felt as a child, and she is now transferring this confusion and pain to the viewer. It is not an entirely pleasant experience despite the film's fascinating structure and narrative.

This pain of the lies and early trauma is particularly felt in the interviews towards the latter part of the film, when the siblings begin to talk about the violence that had ensued in their families after the parents had separated. We realise the reality of the pain the mother too must have felt – as the patriarchal society stripped her of the right to look after her children; she was deemed an unfit mother because she left her first husband for another man. How awful all of this must have been (and indeed must be) for the rest of the family, but would this pain not be made worse by the project of the filmmaker and by making her sisters experience their pain as if they were characters on the screen in a spectacle on public display?

In addition, clearly, not all of these filmic choices can be considered as friendly or empowering gestures *vis-à-vis* her family or the viewer – consciously or otherwise. Through the filmmaking process Polley here appears to be replacing and repairing some things, but she is also *sublimating*, not just her pain but also her *rage* towards a patriarchal world that somehow created these structures in the past in which first her mother, then her family and she herself had to struggle to find their way. It is, in part, in this tension between personal pain and rage, on the one hand, and the impersonal patriarchal symbolic structures on the other, that we can locate the performative and ethical dimensions of *Stories We Tell*.

Sublimation?

Freud, and after him Lacan, famously linked sublimation and language – and the process of talking – to libidinal economy. In Seminar XI, Lacan presents the idea of sublimation in prosaic terms. First, he reminds us of Freud's position: sublimation is an empowering creative activity that satisfies libidinal drive. It is a substitute (for sex) but it is not a repression: it gathers the energy of the drive and channels it into something different than sexual activity:

> Freud tells us repeatedly that sublimation is also satisfaction of the drive, whereas it is *zielgehemmt*, inhibited as to its aim – it does not attain it. Sublimation is nonetheless satisfaction of the drive, without repression. In other words – for the moment, I am not fucking, I am talking to you. Well! I can have exactly the same satisfaction as if I were fucking. That's what it means.
>
> (Lacan 1998: 165–166)

Philosopher Simon Critchley (2007) suggests another way of thinking about sublimation, namely, by using the example of Antigone whom Lacan discusses at length in Seminar VII (1992 [1959–60]). In some philosophical paradigms it would be easy to call Antigone unethical (many people die as a result of her actions, which, in the end, one could say, had a meaning for her more than for the world at large). However, she is ethical within the Lacanian paradigm of being faithful to her commitment – 'no matter what'. One could argue that Sarah Polley's decision to sublimate her pain becomes just such a commitment.

Critchley (and Lacan) makes two points: the first one is in relation to one's desire and pain that is given a creative outcome. The second point is to do with beauty and sacrifice, which is inherent in the sublimation of desire – at least according to Critchley's reading of Lacan's Seminar VII. What is the moral goal of psychoanalysis?: 'the moral goal of psychoanalysis consists of putting the subject in relation to its unconscious desire' (Critchley 2007: 73). This is why the sublimation is so important, for it is the realisation of such desire. In Seminar VII Lacan discusses Antigone, the character who sublimates her trauma through an act that is both beautiful and ethical, as she sublimates the horror and trauma of death and destruction into beauty, that is, into an act of sacrifice. On the surface, there is no great sacrifice to be found in Polley's work and yet something indeed *is* sacrificed: the pretended sense of family unity, the fake harmony that nonetheless worked well for years, the lack of knowledge of the truth of her childhood, all of which became her driving force, her *objet petit a*. But on the other hand, once having arrived at the truth of some sort, trust within the family was destroyed completely, in ways difficult to articulate. One of her sisters comes up with a startling revelation to the question 'has anything happened since you have learnt that Sarah's father is another man?', which of course happened as a part of the filmmaker's project. She answers in the following way: 'No, nothing really. Well, we all got divorced, yes – we all got divorced'. The truth, as uncovered by Polley, is brutal and painful – the lie she presents to the viewer through fake obsolete technology might be a repetition of the lie she and her family had experienced.

In one of his late seminars (XXIII) Lacan introduces the notion of *sinthome*, with which he interprets the process of *writing* (for Joyce) as perhaps more than a form of sublimation. Here, Lacan perceives writing rather as a tool with which one wards off one's descent into mental illness. It prevents psychosis and total chaos through creativity, not particularly by taking the Other into consideration. I have, furthermore, suggested elsewhere (Piotrowska 2014) that a documentary film on occasion could be interpreted as such a *sinthome* for the filmmaker. In Polley's case, the making of the film is perhaps indeed more than the process of sublimation, it is her *sinthome*. The process of this creative work (resulting in a performative documentary) is brutal, for it seems that her taking control and asserting power are more important to her than simply representing the truth that has been uncovered.

I would therefore argue against Elsaesser here who has claimed that via the use of obsolete technology Polley is 'working through' her family issues. I would rather suggest that her use of digital technology is building a *replacement* for the void that her mother's death left the family with. In addition, I argue that any fantasy of a happy and at least semi-ordinary family that may have existed in this family before the film was made and screened, was totally destroyed and that that was done in two contradictory ways: on the one hand by the filmmaker's effort to get to the truth (about her mother's life and abut her own origins) and on the other by the use of the obsolete technology which she has used as a tool of deception.

One could also argue that, while making her film, Polley reclaimed the female agency lost by her mother; it is not so much a *Nachträglichkeit* but rather *Vorwärts-träglichkeit*[2] – the move forward to change the future rather than the past. If the use of fake technology is a tool for Polley's empowerment as well as for her sublimation of her own pain and deception, one has to ask the question whether her film (or filmmaking strategy) is in the end ethically justifiable at all – particularly *vis-à-vis* her family, who willingly participate in the film. In terms of Levinas' 'Infinite Responsibility for the Other' one has to say very clearly that it would be hard to defend this film project as ethical: her own father is shamed and her family is ridiculed; they are seen in tears and deeply upset. The film is a fascinating piece but, in terms of adhering to a responsible stance towards the Other, it is deeply questionable.

Foucault and the act of reviewing of the self

Before I return to Davina Quinlivan's work on reparation in film, I want to suggest another way of thinking about the ethics of *Stories We Tell* – and, more generally, ethics in the documentary encounter. In recent scholarship on documentary film, and indeed in film studies as a whole, Emmanuel Levinas' work on the 'Infinite Responsibility for the Other' (Levinas 1961, 1981) has gained much currency (see for example Cooper 2006; Renov 2004; Cowie 2011 my own work: 2014, 2015 and 2016). If one follows Levinas, an impossible bind is put on the filmmaker, in which her or his responsibility is called upon through the face of the Other – who is both the contributor to the film and also the film's spectator, practically rendering the whole documentary project unethical as the interests of the film's protagonist can be, and very often are, in stark contrast to that of the filmmaker or even the truth itself. We might recall the famous scene in *Shoah* (1985), in which Lanzmann interrogates Abraham Bomba: truth and knowledge demand that he speak, but in fact the act of speaking becomes torture itself.

In a 2017 Society of Cinema and Media Studies (SCMS) conference paper (so far unpublished) (2017), Michael Renov puts the situation as starkly as possible as a choice on the part of the filmmaker: choose between truth and ethics. However, in another unpublished paper also delivered at SCMS in 2017, Kate Rennebohm (taken from her ongoing doctoral thesis on early local cinema reception) points to the process of reviewing that offers those filmed a chance to reflect on who they are.

Can 'reviewing' be an ethical gesture in the documentary encounter?

The 'local cinema', in the early 20th century, involved filming an event and processing the footage quickly so that the people who participated in these events could see themselves later the same day. In her paper and the doctoral thesis, Rennebohm advances the argument that one could think of the process of seeing oneself on screen as a process of 'reviewing the self' in cinema and that that in turn might provide an ethical opportunity for those who have participated in the film. Whilst Rennebohm's work deals specifically with very early cinema (beginning of the 20th century) my contention here is that one could apply these ideas to the ethics of contemporary documentary film, thus moving the debate away from the Levinasian infinite responsibility of the Other. Rennebohm says, 'the phenomenon of local cinema highlights the ways in which cinema from its earliest appearance engaged the concept of the self, affecting and altering the self and its related concepts in the process' (Rennebohm 2017: 2). Rennebohm further deploys here the work of Michel Foucault, laid out in the lectures of the *Collège de France* (Foucault [1978] 2013 and untranslated 1983 lecture). For my own purposes I have also consulted McGushin's discussion of the notion of Foucault's Askesis (2007) and his ideas of an ethical life in which reflective thinking about the self, as one of many practice exercises, is an ethical gesture (ibid.: 36).

For Foucault, ethics takes shape in the historically shifting ground for thought about the nature of the subject and its possibilities for self-relation. Foucault focuses on a notion of practice and discipline rather than knowledge. In particular, he is interested in the practice of 'thinking', reflecting on one's life that draws from ancient Socratic traditions.

In tracing these different ethical epistemes, Foucault grounds the available possibilities of self-relation at least partially in the media of that historical moment. I suggest here that one can deploy the same or a similar argument for the ethics of the *documentary* encounter as a whole and in particular for situations in which the very moment of talking about difficult matters might create, like in Polley's case, a space which has not been created before.

Foucault's remarks on writing as a facet of the ancient ethical paradigm of self-care stresses the importance of creative technology, which allows for a moment of reflection for those involved. Foucault ascertained 'a relation developed between writing and vigilance. Attention was paid to nuances of life, mood and reading, and the experience of self was intensified and widened by virtue of this act of writing' (Foucault 2013: 232–233).

Rennebohm suggests that these kinds of ethical possibilities might have been offered by the early 'local cinema', which was establishing new modes of viewing oneself and thus perhaps inviting one to reflect on different ways of conceptualising the self, altering the possibilities for ethical or self-relation as such. To my mind, if one conceptualises the documentary experience in this fashion for those who observe themselves in a movie, this might present different ethical possibilities outside the impossible Levinasian claim of the 'Infinite Responsibility for the Other'. It might be that the moment of seeing oneself as the Other constitutes the necessary step in the system of 'self-care' and 'vigilance'. If one takes this seriously, the ethics of a documentary encounter could be viewed differently.

These possibilities are indeed present in Polley's *Stories We Tell*. The film opens up a space of self-reflection, the practice of thinking, self-care and vigilance and through that of a chance of arriving at a new subjectivity. This, then, speaks to the issue of the ethics of the documentary project in a different way: rather than focusing on what the filmmaker is going to do to the contributor/participant of the film, it invites these participants to consider her/his speech and image in order to reflect on who they are. The idea of vigilance and reflection offers us an exit from the impasse of discussing the ethics of a documentary in terms of either the instinctual response 'oh that's not right' or of the condemnation of the filmmaker's pursuit of truth, as this pursuit might be different from that of the Other. The Lacanian fidelity to one's desire offers a good remedy for the filmmaker, but not for the Other, who participates in the documentary text. I have written about not giving up on one's desire at length elsewhere (Piotrowska 2014; Piotrowska 2015). But just to remind ourselves it is the notion of the ethical act consisting of 'not giving up on one's desire' 'no matter what' and, once the commitment is made, to be able to be faithful to it 'beyond the limit' as Lacan puts it (Lacan

[1959–60] 1992: 305). In his Seminar VII on ethics Lacan re-introduced the figure of Antigone thus inviting us to re-think ethics. This is a useful trope to think about Polley's undertaking that took her five years to complete 'no matter what' but it does not deal adequately with the position of her family in it – particularly her father. Hence, to my mind, the notions of 'vigilance' and the 'care of the self' are important to consider here: as the documentary text might open a space for self-reflection beyond and above the hurt the process and even the film itself might inflict on those who are in it.

Drawing from Rennebohm's work (2017) but re-framing it, one could suggest that Foucault's work on the ancient Roman and Hellenistic model (in his lecture of 1983) of self-care can introduce a useful framework for understanding a possibility of particular engagement of the self as well as of those who contribute to a documentary film project. The 'care of the self' describes an ethical framework in thought that values attention to the self, and Foucault finds this framework to be variably at work across a broad set of thinkers and writings dating from the 5th century B.C. to the 5th century A.D. (see a discussion of Foucault's idea of care and vigilance also in McGushin 2007: 33–37). In this way of thinking, the goals of focusing on and building the self constituted an essential aspect of one's ability to contribute to the community, to treat others well, and to lead a good life. One would engage what Foucault calls 'technologies of the self', or actions by which one would act on and take responsibility for oneself, in order to achieve these goals. The care of the self exhorted individuals to 'focus on oneself', 'look at oneself', 'attend to oneself', and to 'keep oneself before one's eyes'. Rennebohm suggests that early cinema offered such a space of reflection for the participants of the process – of being filmed and then watching the footage. The ethical part of this process would amount to a notion of deep self-reflection contributing to a desire to improve one's relationship with others (ibid.: 7).

To my mind this is a productive way of thinking about the documentary encounter, even though of course one cannot guarantee that the moment of self-reflection is present in the viewer. Towards the end of the film, Polley has a sequence which exactly seems to evoke the notion of 'reviewing' of the self, in which her interviewees are intercut with each other, looking reflectively and in a forlorn way, into the distance, and, intermittently, at the filmmaker, while perhaps indeed reviewing their actions and words, as well as their part in both the life of the filmmaker and in the film she has created. No words are uttered in that sequence and no words are needed. The faces, filmed in close ups – which remind us of Béla Balázs' (2009: 276) insistence on the importance of close ups in cinema – evoke a sense of vigilance in the viewer; and if that viewer is indeed the person whose face it is, the experience must be pivotal.

Final thoughts

In *Stories We Tell*, the nasty woman in the guise of the filmmaker thus creates a new space, a new body, and this notion, in turn, connects to Quinlivan's link between the 'reparation' work of film (for the spectator) and haptic theory in film studies, advancing the idea that a film's body offers, or can offer, a site for healing ('healing' is Quinlivan's phrase, not a word a Lacanian would use). It connects in particular to the work of Vivian Sobchack, who argues that the

> 'film's body' is not visible in the film, except for its intentional agency and diacritical motion. It is not anthropomorphic, but it is also not reducible to the cinematic apparatus (in the same way that we are not reducible to our material physiognomy); it is discovered and located only reflexively as a quasi-subjective and embodied 'eye' that has a discrete if ordinarily prepersonal and anonymous existence.
>
> (Sobchack 2004: 107–108)

Quinlivan reminds us also that in psychoanalysis, Klein's Freudian theory of reparation examines infantile aggression and anxiety in terms of their constitution of an ambivalent drive towards the destruction and subsequent restoration of the mother's body. For Klein, the mother's breast symbolises the most important *object* the infant encounters; the breast is at once a source of plenitude and frustration that, in turn, becomes an object of love and hate. One could argue therefore that in *Stories We Tell* the filmmaker's decision to adopt the performative documentary mode in order to create her own 'good object', and a new body, through the use of the pretend obsolete technology in the fake archive, is part of this desire to create a different object.

In terms of what the film offers for the participants of the film and its spectators, I have suggested that thinking of the ethics of documentary via Foucault's notion of 'reviewing oneself' is a productive venture. I have borrowed this thought, claiming that it is equally valid to the study of documentary film. I have also suggested that the notion of 'reviewing the self' goes beyond the 'responsibility for the Other' which puts impossible and unfulfillable demands on the filmmaker. Instead, the responsibility is handed back to the participant and the spectator – for 'the reviewing'. This notion gives us a chance to indeed review the notion of ethics in documentary filmmaking and is particularly relevant in the current digital age, where the access to any film work is so very easy.

Considering this in regard to Sarah Polley's *Stories We Tell*, finally it is important to mention that there is a certain repetition of her mother's position between the two men: Polley finds herself torn between the very same men – her fathers – but this time using her film and its language as a vehicle of not just her defence, but, arguably, also as a vehicle of aggression *vis-à-vis* the Name of the Father. In the Oedipal triangle of *Stories We Tell* it is indeed the storytelling, the chosen filmic language, which offers a Lacanian *sinthome*, like a possibility of hanging onto one's sense of the self. It is through dismantling the existing fixed points in her life, the Lacanian *point de capiton*, that Polley is able to begin to build another identity. Her choice of the particular filmic mode (the performative documentary) and particular technology, digital and obsolete, is symptomatic and crucial – and deception that is never completely explained or dismissed, appears to be a part of the filmmaker's reparation of her trans-generational trauma.

As a kind of coda, I would like to share that when I teach this filmic text at my own university in the UK and others internationally, students usually gasp at the realisation of the extent of the deceit that has been presented to them. At a very recent session at the Gdansk University in Poland, where I did a stint as a Visiting Professor in Film, a heated debate ensued verging on a row. It is possible that the country's turn to conservatism and right-wing family values has made the film particularly controversial. One of the students screamed across the room (and let the gender of the student remain a secret): 'there is no excuse for this kind of nastiness'. Personally, I forgive the deceit and applaud it. The film does shift something, not just for that family but for us all. Its unflinching honesty – and I use the word advisedly – in revealing the mechanics of the filmmaking, including its necessary cruelty, without disclosing everything teaches the viewer how to tolerate uncertainty and a lack of rigid binaries that characterises patriarchal systems. This achievement alone by this nasty woman is a great testimony to the filmmaker's integrity and courage.

Notes

1 The paper was given at the British Association for Film and Screen Studies conference in Bristol in April 2017.
2 The term was used first at a summer session of the Nordic Summer University of 2017 in Oriversi, Finland, in a discussion of a short paper I gave on this text with Rafael Dernbach.

Bibliography

Balázs, B. (2009 [1948]) 'The face of things', in Braudy, L., and Cohen, M. (eds.), *Film theory and criticism: Introductory readings.* Oxford: Oxford University Press, pp. 273–281.

Bruzzi, S. (2000) *New documentary: A critical introduction.* London: Routledge.

Cooper, S. (2006) *Selfless cinema? Ethics and French documentary.* Cambridge: Cambridge University Press.

Cowie, E. (2011) *Recording reality, desiring the real.* London and Minneapolis: University of Minnesota Press.

Critchley, S. (2007) *Infinitely demanding: Ethics of commitment, politics of resistance.* London and New York: Verso.

Elsaesser, T. (2014) 'The poetics and politics of obsolescence', keynote at 'The Future of Obsolescence', *9th Orphan Film Symposium*, Amsterdam March 30–April 2, 2014. In German: http://2014.doku-arts.de/content/sidebar_fachtagung/Thomas-Elsaesser.pdf

Foucault, M. [1978] (2013) *Lectures on the Will to Know.* Ed. A. Davidson. Trans. by G. Burchell. New York: Springer.

Foucault, M. (2013) *Lectures on the will to know.* Edited by A. Davidson. Translated by G. Burchell. New York: Springer.

Freud, S. (1958 [1915]) 'Observations on transference-love (further recommendations on the technique of psycho-analysis III)', in *The Standard Edition of the complete psychological works of Sigmund Freud. Volume XII.* Translated by J. Strachey. London: Hogarth Press and the Institute of Psychoanalysis, pp. 157–217.

Lacan, J. (1992 [1959–60]) *Seminar VII: The ethics of psychoanalysis 1959–1960.* Translated by D. Potter. London: Routledge.

Lacan, J. (1998 [1981]) *Seminar XI: The four fundamental concepts of psychoanalysis.* Edited by J.-A. Miller. Translated by A. Sheridan. London and New York: W. W. Norton.

Lacan, J. (2006 [1966]) *Écrits.* Translated by B. Fink. New York: W. W. Norton.

Lebow, A. (2008) *First person Jewish.* London and Minneapolis: University of Minnesota Press.

Levinas, E. (1961) *Totality and infinity.* Translated by A. Lingis. Pittsburgh: Duquesne University Press.

Levinas, E. (1981) *Otherwise than being.* Translated by A. Lingis. The Hague: Martinus Nijhoff Publishers.

McGushin, E. (2007) *Foucault's askesis: An introduction to the philosophical life.* Evanston: Northwestern University Press.

Nichols, B. (1994) *Blurred boundaries: Questions of meaning in contemporary culture*. Bloomington: Indiana University Press.

Oever, A. van den (ed.) (2010) *Ostrannenie*. Amsterdam: Amsterdam University Press.

Piotrowska, A. (2014) *Psychoanalysis and ethics in documentary film*. London and New York: Routledge.

Piotrowska, A. (ed.) (2015) *Embodied encounters: New approaches to psychoanalysis and cinema*. London and New York: Routledge.

Quinlivan, D. (2014) 'Film, healing and the body in crisis: A twenty-first century aesthetics of hope and reparation', *Screen* 55 (1), pp. 103–117.

Rennebohm, K. (2017) 'The local view genre as a medium of the self', *Conference Paper*. SCMS Chicago.

Renov, M. (2004) *The subject of documentary*. Minneapolis: University of Minnesota Press.

Renov, M. (2017) *On Documentary Ethics*. Unpublished paper delivered at the SCMS conference.

Rothman, W. (1998) 'The Filmmaker as hunter', in Grant, B.K., and Sloniowski, J. (eds.), *Documenting the documentary: Close readings of documentary film and video*. Detroit: Wayne State University Press, pp. 23–40.

Sobchack, V. (2004) *Carnal thoughts: Embodiment and moving image culture*. Berkeley: University of California Press.

Soler, C. (2015) *Lacanian affects: The function of affect in Lacan's work*. Translated by B. Fink. New York: Routledge.

Winston, B. (2001) *Lies, damn lies and documentaries*. London: British Film Institute.

4 The *non-femme fatale* in *Red Road*

How could one possibly frame Jackie, the protagonist of *Red Road* (2006) as a *femme fatale*? She seems understated, quiet even. Hers is not the theatrical performativity of a *femme fatale*. She dresses modestly and works hard. The film's language is not that of the noir, either classical or contemporary: Andrea Arnold's film deploys documentary techniques and appears straightforward. This is deceptive, for the world the filmmaker creates is complex and her protagonist a woman who will use her sexuality to influence events. Jackie has a secret and a hidden agenda: she is planning a crime, using a man, who, indeed, following the usual narrative trope of *film noir*, is a stranger in town. Clearly this is not a schema which would take us very far, nonetheless it is worth bearing it in mind as a starting point.

Red Road was Andrea Arnold's first feature film. It won the Jury Prize in Cannes in 2006 and had many interesting critical reviews since its opening.[1] There have been some significant academic analyses of the film (Pisters 2004; Horeck 2011). Most writers were dubious about the lengthy erotic scene in the film and overlooked its significance completely. Arnold's attitude to sex altogether has been criticised; for example, in *Sight and Sound* a viewer wrote: 'the director has thrown it in to give a purposeless script some drive. Frivolous, cheap and not very convincing at all' (Pattison 2009). There is a hesitation in naming the key element in Jackie's trajectory which manages to dislodge her sense of loss and which catapults her out of a virtual desert of an inability to engage with the world. I suggest it is her unexpectedly all-encompassing sexual encounter with Clyde that alters her planned course of action. In the film's narrative it offers a paradigmatic turning point. Far from being straightforward, Jackie's trajectory is complicated and revelatory: it combines many elements and includes the technology of surveillance, the (male and female) gaze and the trauma of loss. It uses a *femme fatale* trope and immediately subverts it. She enters the path of the 'nasty woman' but then is able to change it.

Throughout this chapter I am using the Lacanian notion of *jouissance* to underpin my argument. *Jouissance* – which literally means 'enjoyment' in French – is in Lacanian psychoanalysis a complicated notion, signifying bodily pleasure linked to unconscious desire, to the Real, and therefore to the body but also often to internal and actual prohibition. *Jouissance* is therefore always tainted with pain in some way and is not a straightforward emotion.[2] But in part, I am also doing something else here, attempting yet again to pull together different theoretical paradigms.

Emma Wilson in her writing about Catherine Breillat (2015: 11) does just that beautifully. She calls Breillat's films 'inchoate, ravishing' (ibid.: 11) and then goes on to say: 'for me their wager is to touch some membrane, some limit, between the unconscious and the sensate word' (ibid.: 11). For me this is what Andrea Arnold's first film does – it touches me intellectually (theoretically) but also in a sensory way. Again evoking Wilson's language about Breillat, I offer here a complicit response to the film 'a sensory, imaginative investigation, as I feel my way into her works' (ibid.: 11).

There are some intriguing elements in *Red Road*. Technology plays an important part in this film as does looking and not seeing. One could argue of course that technology is important in *all films noirs* and in the films discussed in this volume in particular: the notion of the crime involves often some form of technology – it is unusual for the victim to be murdered using somebody's bare hands, or sheer physical violence (although indeed this is the case in *Gone Girl*). Usually, there are schemes involving guns, car chases, car crashes and computers. Technology is an actor in *film noir*. In this film, technology is both the initial trigger of events in the meta narrative of the film (the car accident) and also makes things possible at all, for Jackie is a surveillance officer: it is her job to observe other people's lives on CCTV screens. Without this technology the whole premise, storyworld and narrative trajectory of the film would collapse. Jackie sees Clyde (the man who, we eventually discover, killed her husband and child through reckless driving) and hatches her revenge plan when she sees him on her monitor screens.

However, the nasty woman in *Red Road* is transformed by something other than technology or her rage and desire for revenge. Her agency is corrupted by her pain and a sense of betrayal (as it is for Amy in *Gone*

Girl) but here she regains her focus in a most unexpected way – not through the desire to carry out revenge (the usual trope in *film noir*) but rather through the erotic energy that Audre Lorde (2017) writes about. In Andrea Arnold's film it is the character's preparedness to embrace the energy of the erotic encounter that propels the change. Jackie opens herself to this energy, becomes the subject and not the object, and through it allows for the sexual encounter to be an intersubjective meeting which transforms this revenge movie into something else. I will consider the nature of this 'something else' later in this chapter.

It is also worth reflecting briefly on *Red Road* against the backdrop of three films that deal with a very similar incident, namely a tragic car accident. The accident results in the main protagonist, the woman, being left alive, whilst her family, a child and a husband in two cases, and just a child in the case of the third one, die in the crash. The other two films which have a curiously similar starting point in their narratives are Krzysztof Kieslowski's *Three Colours Blue* (1993) (with Juliette Binoche playing the lead) and *Cake* (2014) starring Jennifer Aniston and directed by Daniel Barnz. *Red Road*, however, is bolder and more innovative both in its story telling and final narrative solutions. It is also the only film in this group of cinematic texts written and directed by a woman.

One could say that the narrative of all three films centres on the woman coming to terms with her tragic loss and pain, and finally choosing creativity and life over death. In Kieslowski's *Three Colours Blue* the main character is semi-paralysed and gets re-awakened by two occurrences: rather predictably, by a man she likes and the creative work he is inviting her to share with him, namely finishing her dead husband's musical work. The film, which launched Binoche's career, has been much acclaimed, but has also been criticised for its elaborate and over-aestheticised look. In *Cake* the main protagonist Claire played by Jennifer Anniston is in continuous physical pain. Addicted to painkillers and anti-depressants she is suicidal. Her salvation comes in the guise of her Mexican housekeeper and carer, Silvana, a woman who is a mother figure but also a kind of everyman 'other' who rescues her through language, through a direct approach of telling her she needs her to stay alive because she cares for her. She tells her off for her continuous attempts to kill herself which fill the Mexican carer with horror because she loves her. The expression of this love through language becomes a key element of the broken woman's transformation – or this at least is my reading of the film. *Cake's* protagonist certainly has some kind of agency but it is compromised through her pain. Claire uses her sexuality, too, but she uses it not as a way of communicating with the other but as a Band Aid, offering a very temporary relief and resulting in a deep sense of hopelessness.

Red Road's Jackie suffers a similar loss and she too is disconnected from the world. She finds her agency and her will to re-enter the life of living through, as mentioned previously, first of all a chance encounter facilitated by technology but then an overwhelming bodily engagement with the most unexpected other.

Before her transformative moment takes place, or is engendered by her, Jackie is addicted to a voyeuristic *jouissance* brought about by feelings of omnipotent and illusory power over those she watches on CCTV cameras. The omnipotent fantasy is helpful briefly as it fuels her sense of agency but it does not last as one could venture that it is built on a simulacrum of agency – a pretend situation which cannot last. The notion of the accident is important both in this film and in others in this volume.

It is worth therefore even in passing to mention the notion of technology and the accident in this film (through the work of Paul Virilio). I have discussed this in a different context elsewhere (Piotrowska in Purse 2017) but it is significant to briefly consider how 'an accident' and Lacanian 'fate' are connected but different. Paul Virilio's notion of 'accident' is first set out in *The Original Accident* (2007). Virilio links 'the accident' – and more specifically a technological accident – to a notion of an 'attack'. Virilio proposes that the 20th century swamped us with mass produced accidents one after the other 'from the sinking of the Titanic in 1912 up to the Chernobyl meltdown in 1986' (ibid.: 5). These are linked to humanity's advancement through technology but, he claims, technology and its accidents have also stalled our ethical progress as the value of human life and the body has become less important. This links his earlier work to the patriarchal and the war which not only uses technology but also promotes its advancements, including cinematic technology. In *Red Road* such masculine technology, which ultimately is designed to control and destroy the enemy, is juxtaposed with the body – and more specifically woman's body.

In *Red Road*, as in the other two films mentioned at the outset, the accident is the starting point of the films – not a large-scale technological accident like Titanic or Chernobyl but an ordinary daily technological attack – a car accident which ruins the texture of a family's lives, and which creates traumas one often cannot recover from. The technological accident causes other forms of accident, including those that deal blows to our minds, our psyches, our brains.

It is here also that one could introduce Catherine Malabou's notion of an 'ontology' of accident (2012) – concerning the plasticity of our brains – and our ability to respond to a trauma that our minds can only deal with up to a certain point. Malabou talks about destructive plasticity – i.e. a negative change in the brain which cannot be brought back through *any* means. This she says is the opposite of the psychoanalytical transformation – it is a catastrophic change brought about by brain damage, or dementia or, at times, severe trauma, the effect of which cannot be reversed.

As stated earlier, in *Red Road* the whole action relies on technology – the CCTV cameras enable Jackie to look at the world without being engaged in it. She works for the police and her job is to watch the image. It is her 'addiction' perhaps which covers her profound sense of loss and despair – as a viewer we do not understand why she is the way she is – until much later, perhaps until the very end of the film. We are unclear what might be going on but have a sense that there is something hidden to which we simply are not privy. So the notion of the visible and invisible, the old phenomenological obsession so prevalent in Merleau Ponty's debates with Lacan in Seminar XI, is very present here – it is another take on the familiar binary in *Blue Velvet*, for example, represented by the mess of the worms under the prettiness of the lawn.

There is something strangely obsessive going on in Jackie's watching, observing, looking – it feels almost post-human, meaning that she appears not to need a different kind of contact – she appears detached, not happy but not unhappy either: technology offers her quite a lot, certainly acting as a form of sublimation but it is of a very limited and limiting kind. Suddenly there is another dimension to the technology, namely its ability to produce another 'accident', that of Jackie finding Clyde.

It is very clear that the film draws heavily from a tradition of films in which the key protagonist is also a voyeur – the world out there is different from the world he or she inhabits. The notion of spying on other people was presented and interrogated in classic films such as Hitchock's *Rear Window* (1954), Antonioni's *Blow Up* (1966), Coppola's *The Conversation* (1974) and Kieslowski's *A Short Film about Love* (1988) – to name but a few.

In these films, for a variety of reasons, the main protagonist is separated from the actions which unfold either before their very eyes (*Rear Window* or *The Conversation*) or with some time lapse (*Blow Up*). In all the films the protagonist's position in the actual world is ambiguous – s/he still desires to be a part of it – albeit at a distance. The separation

offers safety but it is also a source of painful confusions as the protagonists get misled by the clues they are given – they misread the signs
and arrive at incorrect conclusions which then have to be corrected, re-
thought through and appropriate actions taken – or not, because perhaps
it is too late to take them.

It might be important to state here the obvious which is vital in our
perception of these films: we are invited to reflect on our own position
as cinema spectators – we too are engaged in the world presented on
screen but somehow can neither influence events in any concrete way
nor be sure that what we have perceived is in fact what is going on the
screen – and very possibly we are completely mistaken, as the characters
in the films mentioned previously, including Jackie in *Red Road*. The
life as watched (or listened to) by the protagonists of the classic films
does invade their private space – in *Red Road* too the private space is
invaded: first, by the compelling desire to take revenge – so the death
drive fuelled by her melancholia – and then by Jackie's invitation to
the stranger to invade her body – which results in something utterly
unexpected.

The key tension of the film remains unresolved – we don't really know
what happens and why. The film does not offer a 'proper' explanation –
just clues. We are still like CCTV spectators – we only know bits of the
world the filmmaker creates.

Some things we do know. The world Jackie observes is like silent
cinema – the screens do not provide any sounds. The crucial notion of
the film is that of seeing and not seeing and hearing and not hearing
but also of being 'inside' and 'outside' – and desiring desperately, consciously or otherwise, to be inside. Significantly, all three women in the
films concerning the loss of the family (*Three Colours Blue* and *Cake* as
well as *Red Road*) do consider using sex with a man – basic penetrative
sex – as a strategy to feel better and to get dislodged from the world of
apathy and pain they feel. In *Three Colours Blue* and *Cake* this strategy
fails. It works in *Red Road* despite the almost perverse setting for the
encounter. There are clearly many reasons for this.

The basic facts of the narrative are probably worth recalling here.
Jackie discovers that a man she thinks she recognises on CCTV cameras
is indeed somebody she knows. The man has been released from prison
on parole. Jackie verifies the facts with her lawyer and then follows the
man to his house, befriends him, meets his flatmates and then ends up
at a party. She dances with the man, whose name is Clyde and somehow begins to desire him. She follows him again. A love scene ensues

Figure 4.1 Sex scene between Clyde (Tony Curran) and Jackie (Kate Dickie) in
           Red Road
(Andrea Arnold 2006)

between them which takes a long time – 'uncomfortably' long time says
one of the critics – after that event, Jackie still tries to frame him for rape,
thus carrying out her original notion of revenge – so that he can be sent
back to prison.

   None of this is stated clearly and the viewer is given clues and bits of
a puzzle. Jackie then changes her mind and withdraws her charges. The
actual motive for her decision is never spelled out in the film. She seeks
Clyde out one last time, stopping him in the street, on his way from the
arrest. He does not want to talk to her but she convinces him to do so by
explaining who she is. Only then do we learn that Clyde was the driver
of a van that drove into her daughter and husband when they were at a
bus stop. He killed them because he was stoned. He tells her the story of
the accident and walks away.

   First, I suggest the success of the sexual encounter which changes
Jackie's life is due to the fact that it has been driven by her unconscious
desire – which is exactly the opposite to Jackie's conscious objective
and her will to frame Clyde and to deliver revenge. Her unconscious
desire appears to be linked to her loss and his connection to it of which
more directly. Her unexpected desire for Clyde is crucial and complex
but the dislodging of her apathy is also achieved, and it needs to be said

straightforwardly and simply, because Clyde is a very generous lover and his lovemaking, which in the film is presented in a famous and long scene, clearly meets Jackie's desire and her drive head on, changing her sense of being 'outside' the living.

In an edited collection coming from a completely different discipline, namely architectural materialism (Tolla-Kelly and Rose 2006) the writers draw our attention to the scene in which Clyde's friend excitedly and unexpectedly asks Jackie and his girlfriend if they 'want to feel the wind'. He throws the window wide open – everybody is taken aback by the strength of the gust. The man lifts his girlfriend up and terrifyingly pretends to push her out of the window. The 'inside' is desirable and safe but without the 'outside' is can be tedious and dead. The writer further mentions the fact that the English term 'window derives from the Middle English vindauga. Eye of the wind (vindr – wind – and auga – eye) the window and the wind' (ibid.: 147). The window is at the core an opening between inside and outside and at the same time bringing it in (Friedberg in ibid.: 113). Friedberg further points out that the opening is always relational – the work that a window does is relative to the walls around it (window to wall ratios and window placement) (ibid.: 120). One cannot separate off the ability of the window to attach itself evermore emphatically and narrowly to the experience of the 'view', from the elaboration of other non-window technologies given over to the management of atmosphere. In *Red Road* the window scene is therefore an apt precursor of the sex scene – the body swept away by desires one begins to have little control over. The screens of Jackie's work are also windows of sorts but her crossing from the 'outside' to the 'inside' happens unexpectedly.

Sex is a political gesture

Social philosopher Drucilla Cornell and her collaborator Stephen D. Seely (her PhD student at the time of the writing) wrote an article entitled 'There's Nothing Revolutionary about a Blowjob' (2014: 1).[3] It refers to the now famous and corruptive gesture on the part of the Soviet revolutionaries who demanded that their fellow female revolutionaries give them blowjobs as a gesture of revolutionary solidarity. There is something interesting to consider about what actually happens in the sexual encounter and its representation on screen. In Hollywood and most art house movies (as opposed to pornography or the excess cinema of Catherine Breillat for example) the scenes do not unfold beyond suggestive kissing and some eroticism, more implied that actual. In pornography – an easily available straight pornography site would offer scenes with men getting blowjobs as the first port of call – of course one can ask for anything and clearly lesbian sex sites would suggest a different experience.[4] On the whole, women are seen offering fellatio more readily than men offering oral sex to women. It is possible that this is to do with the actual physicality of it i.e. what one can actually see – but not entirely. One could argue that it is the matter of power and control too. Interestingly on the free porn sites which I have surveyed for this work, the only women who are being given oral sex are celebrities – such as Paris Hilton in her famous encounter with Rick Salomon. She does of course offer him fellatio too but it is very clearly her choice and after she has been pleasured. In many cultures 'going down on a woman' is still considered unclean. One could say that how you have sex is not just relevant to the culture of the partners, but rather it is still a representation of the power balance in the act. In this respect *Red Road* is exceptional in letting a man pleasure a woman with no reciprocal arrangement either offered, given or expected. The female writer/director clearly portrays the erotic scene in a very particular way: the power is given back to the man for the final stretch of this scene at which point it is very clear that Jackie does not pretend and that her engagement is complete here.

Before the encounter with Clyde, Jackie does not do much. She watches people lives on screens. Her job appears to be alerting the authorities about crimes she might witness. Fairly frequently, she gets things wrong in terms of what is actually taking place on the screen but we can see what she is fascinated by watching – human intimacy, including owners' relationships with pets which she clearly finds touching, or people having sex, somehow getting close to each other, even in ugly quick encounters, on the streets of the council estate she watches.

The shots of Jackie looking at the screens at work, the close ups of her face, the close ups of her hand caressing at times the control panels evoke a sense of loneliness – behind the screens, outside of the physical or emotional closeness in front of her. Her own sex life appears very limited, not to say basic – but it does exist. We see her having a very quick encounter in a car, with a married colleague. She seems detached during that encounter too – hardly noticing it. The man says 'I can never tell with you. Did you?' 'Yes, yes' she says and we know she is lying. They are both fully dressed and the encounter is absurdly short. We see a stranger passing by, having just peed by the side of the road: doesn't this indicate that Arnold suggests a sexual encounter of the kind Jackie is having just now is similar to going to the loo? Perfunctory, basic, physi-ological, biological – boring Jackie at all times appears to go through the motions of life, without actually living it. If the film in part is a metaphor for being catapulted out of the feeling of being 'outside' to an 'inside', then Arnold makes sure that the viewer does not confuse any sexual encounter with the sense of being 'inside'. Clearly, the point is not that cunnilingus is the key to female sexual pleasure as it is very possible to have highly rewarding sex without it: the point is that in this film the whole way the encounter is presented in a long sequence is that it ruptures the narrative as we have followed it hitherto, and that it opens up its storyworld. For a number of reasons in this narrative Clyde drags Jackie from the outside, inside – her unconscious desire and her body having a major part to play in this event. I venture here that the filmmaker drags the viewer into a different mode of perceiving the film, evoking the visceral experience of the scene and evoking haptic film theorists, of which more later. The viewer cannot remain in the position of the observer alone. The scene's power lies in moving the spectator from the outside in, the skin of the film touching the skin of the audience, the gesture which has aroused complicated responses.

If we take a step back, we remind ourselves how the film's driving force is Jackie's discovery of a man on CCTV cameras – again we under-stand that he is somehow connected to her life – and that he has been released on parole instead serving 10 years. It is this piece of informa-tion which propels Jackie to seek him out – and she does, little by little, entering a world she has previously chosen not to be part of any more.

Ranjana Khanna (2003) in her influential book *Dark Continents* uses the psychoanalytical term 'melancholia' to denote a state infused by agency – sometimes destructive. She evokes Freud's *Mourning and Mel-ancholia* as two different 'responses to a loss'. She reminds us that 'what distinguishes melancholia is a state of dejection, and a form of critical agency that is directed toward the self' (ibid.: 21). She also reminds us of the difference between mourning as 'assimilating [of the lost object] – and melancholia – swallowing the lost object as whole' (ibid.: 21). The difference of Khanna's approach to the traditional approach is the insis-tence that melancholia could carry within itself an agency which might be destructive to the outside world – and not only to the self. Addiction for example could be viewed therefore as a response to a profound mel-ancholia, a sense of loss which is not correctable or retrievable, an act of dramatic and violent defiance against the world which had caused this loss to occur. I have used Khanna's work elsewhere (Piotrowska 2014,

2015) as I find the description of melancholia as powerful instead of just debilitating an intriguing intervention.

I am invoking it here again to theorise Jackie's destructive drive vis-à-vis Clyde – (in the other two films vis-à-vis the protagonists themselves). Khanna reminds us that a way *out of* the violence of melancholia is through 'metaphorisation' of the pain and to a certain extent the other two women protagonists suffering from melancholia (in *Cake* and in *Three Colours Blue*) do just that – through language and images with the Other their pain is alleviated. Not so in *Red Road*.

Jackie's state of ontological destructive paralysis is reversed in the first instance by her destructive desire to carry out revenge on Clyde – a destructive act as described by Khanna. The action is indeed a planned violence – again as described by Khanna: Jackie wants to frame Clyde for rape by first seducing him and then performing violence on her own body in order to demonstrate a fake crime he did not commit. But second, and most important, her bodily feminine *jouissance*, the *jouissance* which needs the Other to produce a satisfaction, creates a revelatory rupture that unexpectedly catapults her out of her inability to feel and be in the world. Lacan tells us that the phallic *jouissance*, or the enjoyment enjoyed by a man (and we need to bear in mind here that Lacan has no time for biology), is a masturbatory experience with no need for the Other.

The feminine *jouissance* which for Lacan is the far fuller experience is something only a woman can experience – not every woman and not always but on occasions. It is a joy fuelled by (the unconscious) desire for the Other which can find momentary fulfilment in the Real – in the body, outside the language but connected to it by unconscious desire. This kind of *jouissance* is hard to write about and theorise as it is not really about love but has shades of love (see Lacan in Seminar XX and Fink's discussion of the Other *jouissance* (in Fink 1997: 106–110)). In *Red Road* it is about deep bodily satisfaction that comes from the man whom she is trying to harm but whom she unconsciously desires. That desire is deeply problematic for her too – she throws up when she first becomes aware of it. She does not want to want him – but she does. She clearly convinces herself she can control that desire and carry out the revenge and she does begin to – but something else happens too.

In Lacan desire is always connected to knowledge: the question here is what kind of knowledge Jackie might be after? We do not know. Arnold leaves clues but no clear suggestions. Yet it seems – and is confirmed by the final scene discussed earlier – that Jackie's desire is connected to the knowledge that links to her loss; Clyde does have the knowledge Jackie might want, the dark disturbing knowledge which only he has – of the very last moment of her family's life. Through the language they exchange, which begins to build Jackie's desire, Clyde also shares intimate information about his own life, including his commitment to abandon forever his own addictions – for a number of reasons but also because he too has a daughter, a teenage daughter whom he still hopes he could be a father to. This revelation that he too has a daughter he has lost but could perhaps re-gain is important. The two people, Jackie and Clyde, the woman removed from the world of the living and the man who inadvertently through his addictions killed her family, make an impossible and brief but deeply significant connection – through their conversations and ultimately their lovemaking. Arnold makes it very clear in her film that these conversations alone do not produce the shift of Jackie's attitude to Clyde; it is the profound physical connection, fuelled by Jackie's unconscious desire that does it. It is here that a further question is worth asking:

Would it be possible to theorise further the significance of the erotic encounter, removing it from gender binaries? Would the erotic power of the film which in some way touches the viewer too be felt in a more extreme circumstance?

Tentacular thinking

> The tongue, this invertebrate, which is the grey eminence of Amorpolis, is the prime minister in the shadow cabinet; in fact, much more capable than the officially serving Penis; the tongue is so underestimated. And yet he can do everything! Wedge anywhere, in the mouth, in the ear, under the eyelid, under the armpit, in the groin, bore into the nest between the thighs, ring the bell near the door of your sex, detect the smallest response, dance every dance, swim, grind, irritate, apologize, smooth, clean up. He can even ejaculate; a well-trained tongue can do it too! The tongue is the real ruler of the world of love. Penis is a servant, rarely clever, more often not very bright. He turns up to finish off the basic job. But the tongue! The real castration wouldn't be the cutting off of the testicles, or a decapitation of the penis, but a loss of the tongue. A man who has lost his tongue has lost his speech and his Eros. He has lost his mind. It is a husk that knows the world only by hearing. What one would call a sophisticated erotic philosophy, is expressed in the tongue of the tongue. I love this tongue.
>
> (Janko 2012: 25)

The preceding passage is from a 2012 novel by the Polish poet and writer Anna Janko – the book, which is a reflection on the overwhelming

power of a sexual encounter, includes paragraphs that testify to the difficulty of writing about sexuality, particularly as experienced by a woman.
That I have chosen a passage focusing on the tongue is no accident here,
as I have mentioned previously but also for other reasons. Janko created a bold novel, particularly as it was written in the now profoundly
conservative and religious Poland. It celebrates the power of a deep sexual bond, outside marriage arrangements, which comes out of a vague
longing that everybody is familiar with, and that here becomes real and
embodied. Also, and it is perhaps too obvious to spell out, the passage
dislodges heteronormative ideas of sex, despite mentioning the penis –
as clearly the tongue, which Janko sees as the king of the erotic realm,
is available to all.

A deep sexual experience is part of being human and has been
thought about and written about for as long as we have been able to
formulate thoughts in language. It is often confused with simple sexual pleasure or even love: while it has elements of both it is neither.
These ephemeral moments of sexual passion of such intensity are rare
despite the apparent plethora of opportunities for erotic adventures in
the contemporary world. The moments of great physical union can be
transformative, and this ability to transform also carries an inherent
sense of risk of being consumed by it, of becoming changed beyond
any recognition, with no chance of turning back. In what follows I
offer a few reflections on the notion of transformation through bodily
fusion introducing a brief discussion of another film which, because
of its non-human element, is well positioned to be an example of the
project of getting rid of a binary through the erotic energy. The film
I want to mention here in passing is *The Untamed* (2016) – in which
the notion of sexual *jouissance* is taken out of the sexual difference
because it takes place between an alien and humans.

The Untamed occupies a space between the horror movie, science
fiction and a gritty urban realism. It focuses on the absolute commitment to the moment and its potential for subsuming and consuming all-
encompassing euphoria through a sexual encounter – a euphoria which
can be seen as embodying Lacanian *jouissance*, and is as transformative
as it is dangerous. In a forest, just outside the city, in a house guarded
by an elderly couple there is an extra-terrestrial creature, which, it is
revealed in the course of the movie, is a huge octopus-like being that
can and does give an otherworldly pleasure to anybody who *chooses* to
enter its space. The choosing is important. This is not a predatory being,
this is not the scenario of Jonathan Glazer's *Under the Skin* where the
alien embodied by Scarlett Johansson prowls the city looking for lonely

men. Their sexual longing is exploited in *Under the Skin* but there is no physical gratification – or any other gratification for that matter as the seduced men disappear into an oblivion of blackness, never to be seen again, their internal organs dissolved. The turning point in the narrative of *Under the Skin* comes when the woman, in her ploy to seduce a disabled man, invites him to *touch* her face and hands as she drives him to her alien lair. Apparently because of the touch, she is unable to destroy him and instead we see her own desire emerge. The touch is important. The philosopher Jacques Derrida in his discussion of Jean-Luc Nancy's essay *Corpus* (2008), reminds us that to touch means 'to tamper with, to change, to displace, to call into question; thus, it is invariably a setting in motion, a kinetic experience' (2005: 25). The touching, therefore, is a harbinger of change – it can be a good change, or bad, but it is a movement, and it can become explosive and revolutionary.

In *The Untamed*, as opposed to *Under the Skin* (2014), there is no element of seduction coming from the Other. The desire comes from the subject who seeks out the creature's abode, succumbing to her or his longing in order to experience the all-embracing pleasure and a fusion with the non-gendered Other. Once a person decides to enter the house where the octopus-like large alien resides (and when I say 'large', I mean elephant-large) she or he is first treated to a mind-altering experience, before entering into a voluntary sexual encounter with the alien creature. People turn up in the lair usually encouraged by stories of the experience – the creature's fame spreads by word of mouth. The nature of the pleasure is consummate and connects to the subject's innermost sexual fantasies and desires. The danger of the encounter appears to come from a sense of merging. To put it differently, those who experience the physical euphoria with the alien often lose all sense of drawing a boundary between them and it, the creature. It seems – which is not made clear – that if only you can pull back in time yourself, no harm will come to you – but the issue is the ability to pull back, when all you want is more – and more. The encounter therefore has the structure and dynamic of addiction.

In *The Untamed*, as in *Red Road*, the urban space is a hostile and mundane environment in which the very texture of the city seems under threat. Veronica, the woman we meet at the beginning of the film, draws us into the city after her accident with the creature. She befriends the male nurse, Fabian, who we learn is having a homosexual affair with a man married to his sister, Ale. Ale and her rough husband Angel have two young children too, suggesting a trans-generational passing on of the restrictions, limitations and abuse. In addition to his adultery with his brother in law, Angel appears to be arrogant, violent and a bad father. After a series of revelations told in a slow, low-key, realistic mode, almost stifling the viewer, the betrayed wife is led to the house in the forest by Veronica. A move away from the city to a forest where the creature lives is significant for its move away from the urban. One of the guardians of the creature tells Ale that in the first instance her mind will be transported – presumably by the powers of the alien, before the pleasure is entered into. Rather like in *Red Road* the move is from 'the outside' in. The first encounter is very successful. The wife feels liberated through her pleasure, through the all-subsuming encounter that, as she explains to her friend, leaves her feeling happy 'when all resentment and hate are gone'. When her violent husband seeks reconciliation, she rejects it saying that she feels well for the first time in her life, and begins dragging him through the forest to the creature so that he too can experience the liberating euphoria. However, it becomes clear when they get there, that further deaths have taken place, as the *jouissance* that dissolved all boundaries has destroyed the lives of new subjects.

It is not that the creature is inherently evil, as opposed to the inexplicably predatory *femme fatale* of *Under the Skin* – where for the record, no sex actually takes place between the alien woman and the annihilated men: the promise of sex is a pure ploy to destroy. In *The Untamed*, on the other hand, the desire comes from the longing subject and is realised beyond any imagination on the part of the recipient who perhaps because of it cannot keep it within reasonable boundaries. This is indeed the territory of the death drive, first mentioned by Freud in his ground-breaking and still controversial publication *Three Essays on the Theory of Human Sexuality* (1953 (1905)) and developed in *Beyond the Pleasure Principle* (1955 (1920)).

In 'The Resistances to Psychoanalysis' (1961), Freud links his notion of sexuality to destruction and danger. It is in this context that he mentions Plato's *Symposium* (1997), a treatise in which the Greek philosopher Socrates and his guests talk about physical love:

> what psychoanalysis calls sexuality was by no means identical with the impulsion towards a union of the two sexes or towards producing a pleasurable sensation in the genitals; it had far more resemblance to the all-inclusive and all-embracing love of Plato's *Symposium*.
>
> (1961: 218)

The film acknowledges the quality of an intense sexual encounter but also recognise its potentially transformative powers with its profound and real risks. The change this kind of *jouissance* brings forth is as inevitable as the risk: it can shatter one's identity and way of thinking, one's status quo, and one's very existence. At times this bodily fusion, the intense giving and taking, *jouissance*, carries with it the risk of self-destruction. The mechanism inherent in *jouissance* was first described by Freud who called it the death drive, a drive which makes us pursue things to the point of destruction, but which also can make us feel more alive than ever – perhaps through our desire to forget the finite quality of all nature's experience – finite because mortality is always a part of it. It is worth it to reflect further on connections between what we mean by love, and what might be understood by deep sexual satisfaction.

In Plato's *Symposium*, the female priestess Diotima explains to the young Socrates what the older Socrates will explain to his dinner companions and to us: namely, that Eros is neither a god nor a mortal, but a *daemon*, an intermediary and hybrid who unites and binds together all separate spheres. This as an idea holds a promise and a threat – the 'binding' heralds a change, a submission to the Other, a union which can have catastrophic consequences as well as exhilarating ones – for if we are to be bound to another being, we lose our separateness; in fact, we lose who we are, our identity. It is this ancient idea of a *daemon* of sensuous desire that one cannot control, which is both life-giving and also potentially fatal, that we observe in *The Untamed*.

I can now return to *Red Road* and the nasty woman in it who is first of all paralysed by her loss, then awoken by a desire to carry out revenge and finally transformed into a woman prepared to enter the world again. Clyde, like the monstrous creature, rather unexpectedly awakens Jackie's desire. He becomes her *objet a* which in Lacan (1999: 63) is not an object of desire but the object-cause of desire, and it is so because it stands in for not something lost, but for 'lostness', the 'goneness' of the absent object, and not the object as such.[5] It is crucial here to understand that there is never any question of replacement for Jackie, no possibility of a relationship. Their encounter and her courage to embrace it is a momentary gift which nonetheless, like in *The Untamed*, is overwhelmingly meaningful and powerful.

As mentioned, *Red Road* draws heavily from a genre tradition where the key protagonist is also a voyeur – the world out there is different from the world he or she inhabits. It is the notion of a division between *inside* and *outside* which demands to be crossed. In Krzysztof Kieslowski's

A Short Film about Love (1988) a young man develops a sexual obsession which he calls love with an older sexually active woman who lives
opposite. In it, the character's sexual longing gets destroyed by the
actual physical encounter with the subject of his infatuation: the fantasy is destroyed by its enactment. Not so in *Red Road* or indeed *The
Untamed* – the encounter with the fantasy works because of the exceptional meeting of the desire, *objet a*, and the body, the drive, because of
the momentary abandonment of all restrictions imposed by the external world – because of, as Plato would say, the miracle of a Temporal
Object, which does involve the body and the mind in one space. As it is
a miracle, it does not take place routinely. It is exceptional.

As mentioned previously, Lacan claims that desire is always connected to knowledge. In Lacan, because of our innate lack and via our
fantasy, we desire those who have what we do not have. Or rather we
desire those who we think might have the knowledge that we lack. In
The Untamed the alien creature has the knowledge to transport anybody
out of the pain of their mundane life, so their relationship to the world
would be 'without hate or resentment', subsumed in a union with the
alien creature, or perhaps rather with one's own embodied fantasies. The
film offers a warning which is not quite present in *Red Road*.

Without wanting to and meaning to, the physical intimacy between
Jackie and Clyde, changes everything for Jackie. That intimacy is made
palpable to the spectator by the long foreplay including indeed lick-
ing of her body as well as through oral sex, with the tongue (as Anna
Janko would have it) being the chief instrument of her desire. Against
Jackie's conscious plan, the encounter becomes an erotic experience,
which wipes out anything else, and as in *The Untamed*, it subsumes
those participating in it. Nobody dies in the encounter but certain things
can never be the same: Jackie loses control completely and there is no
turning back. What does die in the encounter, is the need for the revenge:
the window through which the gust of the wind of life can come in has
indeed been opened and the possibility of life 'inside' once more begins
to be a reality.

What makes the film so potent is Arnold's bold reclamation of the
power of the female body as a site of reconciliation and nourishment
in the middle of a film about loss and revenge. It becomes a film about
feminine *jouissance* and forgiveness. That bodily encounter changes
everything – including the way Jackie thinks. In terms of our discussions on the nasty woman, it is important to state that the transformation
is able to take place because the person in charge is at all times Jackie:

she is always the subject and not the object, in strong contrast to the original *femme fatale* construction. On the side of the viewer, one needs to recognise different emotions that this film can evoke. In the chapter on *Gone Girl* I mentioned anger and rage. Here the emotions are more complex and the haptic film theory and its ideas of visceral approaches to cinema might be helpful to consider, even in conclusion to this chapter. The work of Jennifer Barker (2009), Laura Marks (2000), Vivian Sobchack (2004), Davina Quinlivan (2012) and Emma Wilson (2015) has done much to bring bodily subjectivity to the viewing experience. In her book *The Tactile Eye* (2009), Jennifer Barker evokes the eroticism of some of the film viewing and the following comment I find pertinent to my own experience of watching *Red Road* and a suitable note on which to end this chapter:

> In the palpable tactility of the contact between the film's skin and the viewer's skin, and in the extent to which that contact challenges traditional notions of film and viewer as distant from one another, the tactile relationship between the film and the viewer is fundamentally erotic. Film and viewer come together in a mutual exchange between two bodies who communicate their desire, not only for the other but for themselves, in the act of touching.
>
> (Barker 2009: 34)

Red Road remains a radical gesture despite the years which have elapsed since its making. It challenges the traditional notions of an angry woman as well as a relationship between the film and the viewer. It also challenges and undermines the accepted notions of what might be possible in a cinematic narrative – and in life. It offers hope.

Notes

1 In a very thoughtful review, Jonathan Romney wrote: '*Red Road* emerged out of a Scottish-Danish initiative called Advance Party, co-devised by sometime Dogme director Lone Scherfig, in which three filmmakers were provided with a list of recurring characters. Arnold's opening episode of the trilogy is so powerfully self-enclosed that with all respect to the other two directors, you can't help feeling she's pretty much rendered the rest of the project redundant'. www.independent. co.uk/arts-entertainment/films/reviews/red-road-18-422116.html

2 Lacan uses *jouissance* throughout his oeuvre. For an explanation see for example Fink (1997) but a succinct review of Lacan's different re-formulations of the category *jouissance* can be found in Dylan Evans (1996: 91).

3 Here is the abstract of Cornell and Seely's article: The authors of this article attempt to re-think the relationship between queer theory and Marxism, in order

to argue for a revolutionary queer politics. First, they challenge the idea, offered most forcefully by queer theorist Lee Edelman, that any politics that hopes and struggles for a different future is inevitably a heteronormative project. To respond to this line of thought, this article offers a different approach to the question of futurity and inheritance through a substantive re-reading of Jacques Lacan. At the heart of the authors' analysis, however, is their claim that we need to re-think the relationship between Foucault and Marx so as to return Foucault to a thinker of revolution in all its complexity. The authors then turn to Foucault's deeply misunderstood involvement in the Iranian Revolution to argue that Foucault did not endorse a conservative clerical takeover, but rather saw in the mass uprisings, deeply embedded in Shi'ism, a kind of 'political spirituality' that is necessary to any re-thinking of revolution, but that has been largely lost in Euro-American socialist politics. This political spirituality involves precisely the reconfiguration of 'bodies and pleasures' that Foucault famously calls for in *The History of Sexuality*. Foucault demonstrates, in other words, that a re-thinking of sexuality must accompany any thinking of revolution, but that there can be no autonomous 'sexual revolution' independent from the struggle against capitalism. The article concludes with a discussion of the relationship between the authors' interpretation of Foucault and contemporary attempts to re-think queerness within a Marxist critical frame.
    https://read.dukeupress.edu/social-text/article-abstract/32/2%20(119)/1/
33775/There-s-Nothing-Revolutionary-about-a-Blowjob
4 It is perhaps inappropriate for me to offer links to porn sites which I have visited in the course of doing this research but they are easily available.
5 Elizabeth Cowie elaborates on this further in her new and as yet unpublished essay on Femininity and Psychoanalysis to be published in the new book on the same subject, a volume that I am editing with Ben Tyrer for Routledge to be published in 2019.

Bibliography

Barker, J. (2009) *The tactile eye: Touch and the cinematic experience*. Berkeley: University of California Press.

Cornell, D., and Seely, S. D. (2014) 'There's nothing revolutionary about a blowjob', *Social Text* 32 (2), pp. 1–23.

Derrida, J. (2005 [2000]) *On touching: Jean-Luc Nancy*. Translated by C. Irizarry. Stanford: Stanford University Press.

Evans, D. (1996) *An introductory dictionary of Lacanian psychoanalysis*. New York: Routledge.

Fink, B. (1997) *The Lacanian subject: Between language and jouissance*. Princeton: Princeton University Press.

Fink, B., and Barnard, S. (2012) *Reading seminar XX: Lacan's major work on love, knowledge, and feminine sexuality*. New York: SUNY Press.

Freud, S. (1955 [1920]) 'Beyond the pleasure principle', in *The Standard Edition of the complete psychological works of Sigmund Freud: Volume XVIII*. Translated by J. Strachey. London: Hogarth Press and the Institute of Psychoanalysis, pp. 7–64.

Freud, S. (1961 [1925]) 'The resistances to psychoanalysis', in *The Standard Edition of the complete psychological works of Sigmund Freud: Volume XIX*. Translated by J. Strachey. London: Hogarth Press and the Institute of Psychoanalysis, pp. 213–222.

Horeck, T. (2011) *The new extremism in cinema*. Edinburgh: Edinburgh University Press.

Janko, A. (2012) *Pasja wedlug Swietej Hanki*. Warsaw: Wydawnictwo Literackie.

Khanna, R. (2003) *Dark continents: Psychoanalysis and colonialism*. Durham: Duke University Press.

Lacan, J. (1998 [1981]) *Seminar XI: The four fundamental concepts of psychoanalysis*. Edited by J.-A. Miller. Translated by A. Sheridan. London and New York: W. W. Norton.

Lacan, J. (1999 [1975]) *Seminar XX: On feminine sexuality, the limits of love and knowledge*. Edited by J.-A. Miller. Translated by B. Fink. London and New York: W. W. Norton.

Lorde, A. (2017) *Your silence will not protect you: Essays and poems*. London: Silver Press.

Malabou, C. (2012) *The ontology of the accident*. London: Wiley Blackwell.

Marks, L. (2000) *The skin of the film: Intercultural cinema, embodiment, and the senses*. Durham: Duke University Press.

Nancy, J.L. (2008) *Corpus*. Translated by R. Rand. New York: Fordham University Press.

Patricia, P. (2014) 'The neurothriller', *New Review of Film and Television Studies* 12 (2), pp. 83–93.

Pattison, M. (2009) 'Fish stank', *Sight and Sound* 19 (12), p. 96 (letters page).

Piotrowska, A. (2014) *Psychoanalysis and ethics in documentary film*. London and New York: Routledge.

Piotrowska, A. (ed.) (2015) *Embodied encounters: New approaches to psychoanalysis and cinema*. London and New York: Routledge.

Piotrowska, A. (2017) '"5,000 feet is the best": Drone warfare, targets and Paul Virilio's "Accident"', in Hellmich, C., and Purse, L. (eds.), *Disappearing war: Interdisciplinary perspectives on cinema and erasure in the post-9/11 world*. Edinburgh: Edinburgh University Press, pp. 34–55.

Pisters, P. (2004) *The Neurothriller* in New Review of Film and Television Studies Publication 30 Jan 2014. Doi: 10.1080/17400309.2014.878153.

Plato (1997) *Symposium and the death of Socrates*. Translated by T. Griffith. Ware: Wordsworth Editions Limited.

Quinlivan, D. (2012) *The place of breath in cinema*. Edinburgh: Edinburgh University Press.

Sobchack, V. (2004) *Carnal thoughts: Embodiment and moving image culture*. Berkeley: University of California Press.

Tolla-Kelly, D.P., and Rose, G. (eds.) (2006) *Visuality/materiality: Images, objects, practices*. New York: Routledge.

Virilio, P. (2007 [2005]) *The original accident*. London: Polity.

Wilson, E. (2015) 'Catherine Breillat and Courbet's *L'Orine du monde* (*The origin of the world*) (1866)', in Piotrowska, A. (ed.), *Embodied encounters: New approaches to psychoanalysis and cinema*. London: Routledge, pp. 11–21.

Conclusion

Where else will the nasty woman go – final nomadic remarks

On 25th May 2018 Harvey Weinstein was arrested in New York on the charges of rape and indecent assault (forcing a woman to perform fellatio on him).[1] He was handcuffed and led to a court in New York. In the photo there is an image of the female police detective Keri Thompson, in charge of the investigation into his offences, the woman who did not give up on getting enough evidence for this moment to take place: one of the tweets called her 'badass' – which was meant as a compliment.[2] There was one nasty woman who kept going to get this man who abused his power so horrendously and so sadly (given that he was one of the representatives of the 'dream factory', and co-founder of The Weinstein Company, a film studio involved in so many films we admire and love).

This was a triumphant moment for those who have reported him originally and for many others who did not believe that this moment could ever take place. This was a triumphant moment because many of his victims and many of those who were tactically compliant with Weinstein never believed he would be brought to justice at all. If his actions humiliated and subjugated many women, this image of him being so totally de-throned and brought down would have pleased many. In the many tweets that followed the photo the image of the detective was hailed as a symbol of the actual enforcement of the fight against male oppression.

I must confess I had mixed feelings looking at the photo: I was delighted of course at Weinstein getting his punishment against the odds. I felt really moved that he was led out by a woman representing the law. I was also sad that his monstrous activities had been allowed to go on for so very long and that the best we as society can do is to mete out punishments without correcting the system. His arrest felt exceptional and that felt good but it also felt limited and limiting. This challenging of the male entitlement is necessary. That that person was responsible or at least co-responsible for many films we all respect and even love is near incomprehensible as it would suggest that he was more than just a monster, that he was also a talented and sensitive human being whose darker side, hidden by the system that allows that darkness, took over at times. It is clear that structural changes to the system are necessary with the new movements that build on the #MeToo campaign (such as Timeisup etc). It is also very clear that that the project of imagining of a new world is not an easy one.

The nasty woman is necessary to undermine and defeat the patriarchal power – in cinema and culture as much as in society – but very clearly the necessity of bringing these utterly despicable men to justice is but one part of the story. Because for the world to change in a substantial and positive way, clearly bridges need to be built, awareness altered for good and alliances of many kinds created. The first step is justice – and sometimes even revenge but this does not lead us yet out of the binary in which the men do violence to women and the women do violence to men as retaliation. The redressing of power balance is highly necessary but for it to take place more than an image of a Hollywood mogul brought to account is called for, however much this is a good thing. It is a good thing but it is not enough.

It is here the work of Rosi Braidotti and Donna Haraway is important. Right now we are so traumatised by the patriarchal violence that it is nearly impossible for us to envisage a different cultural constellation. When I say 'us' here I mean everybody. We are conditioned to thinking that violence and power is the only truly effective tool in the contemporary world despite the words of healing and reconciliation. It is very clear that Harvey Weinstein and others must be brought to justice, but my reflection on seeing the image was that of great sadness that our only and indeed correct response to this violence can be a further violence and humiliation – a humiliation which is right and proper and might indeed serve as a deterrent for others but nonetheless is a sad reminder of the world we live in.

The nasty woman in the guise of Rose McGowan and others brought down the monster of Harvey Weinstein and others but there are many more out there, in position of power and authority. These women's bold and decisive gesture was a necessary condition for the invisible but somehow acceptable in the film and other industries was called to a halt. In this volume we can see how the nasty woman in cinema too has created ruptures and sabotaged the established systems of patriarchal might through different means, usually to a great cost to herself: Maya in *Zero Dark Thirty* lives an ascetic lonely life in the bastions of masculine violence, giving up it seems any human relationships outside her work which becomes a relentless pursuit, more a mission than a job. Sarah Polley in *Stories We Tell* reclaims her agency through creating a space in which she is in utter control of the proceedings. She takes charge of the narrative of her own origins through putting her own family on public display and through hurting the man who brought her up on his own for so many years. I claimed in my chapter that she does create a reparative space for herself, with little considerations for the others. I discussed the pathological revenge in *Gone Girl* and *Girl on the Train*, which we can defend as a creative metaphor for rage and revenge vis-à-vis the masculine abuse and violence but which is deeply controversial and uncomfortable too. *Red Road,* which was made in 2006, still feels radical in its narrative in the creation of the main character as it offers an unusual way out of the rage, through a deep erotic encounter with the man perceived as the abuser and, who, however much sympathy we do feel for him, was responsible for the death of Jackie's family. The film – the oldest in this volume – has caused consternation amongst critics and scholars. Its proposition, which one can read as a metaphor proposing the erotic energy rather than violence as a way forward in the world, has not been exactly taken up as a tool either in culture or in the cinema. One could also argue that it is nothing particularly new as the mantra 'make love not war' has been around since the liberalisation of sexual habits since the 60s. Here through Audre Lorde's idea as I understand it is for women to grab the energy which comes from their bodies, including their sexuality, and use it for their own empowerment.

In recent times there have been a number of cinematic texts in which the nasty woman becomes an important protagonist, changing the structures of the encounters even though she does not remain victorious or unscathed. Interestingly, some of these texts are indeed based on actual lives by women. These include *I, Tonya* (2017), *Molly's Game* (2017), *Three Billboards Outside Ebbing, Missouri* (2018) – the powerful women in these films undermine structures of patriarchy through deploying the tools patriarchy has known for centuries. They are not *femme fatales* but they are pretty nasty. *Three Billboards* offers a fabulous Oscar winning performance by Frances McDormand but it is outside the brief of this volume – the main character is a nasty woman of an older kind: her rage fuelled by a horrendously violent crime against her daughter who had been raped and killed. In addition, the film's complicated politics have been the subject of ardent debates and the work certainly does not offer any ways of looking outside the paradigms of violence and revenge. Instead, its presentation of white male racism being redeemed can be seen as deeply problematic.[3] Nonetheless it is important to note that the character's strength is exceptional even if the storyworld and some of the narrative solutions appear somewhat conservative. *I, Tonya* tells a fictionalised story of a figure skater who comes from an underprivileged background with a difficult and abusive mother (and no father) and then is locked into an abusive relationship with her boyfriend and then husband. The narrative follows Tonya's real and perceived difficulties within a sport which traditionally did not allow women from a working-class background into their midst. The brilliant performance by Margot Robin offers a poignant portrayal of a woman who has the talent and the determination but her agency is thwarted by the patriarchal systems determined to keep the status quo intact. The film's experimental structure, which uses pseudo-documentary interviews alongside more traditional dramatic scenes, offers an innovative and radical gesture in its message and its story telling. Another nasty woman in it or rather the performances which embodies it, the mother character who portrays a further take on corrupted female agency, was awarded the Best Supporting Actress Award at 2018 Oscar ceremony.

One can argue that *Molly's Game* offers a reverse side of the *I, Tonya* narrative: the main character begins as a super successful athlete from the right background but her agency is corrupted by a skiing accident. Her competitiveness is in part a gesture against her powerful academic father. The film made by a male director but indeed based on the autobiography written by Molly Bloom states clearly its ambition to dismantle the Oedipal tale as a structure, which a Hollywood film usually follows in terms of a basic coupledom. The character of Molly played brilliantly by Jessica Chastain (who of course played Maya in *Zero Dark Thirty*) in a conversation with her father, a professor of psychology and also a psychotherapist, makes fun of Freud and his ideas of women. The father offers the much-criticised interpretation of Molly's behaviour in the world of high-class poker – namely that she wanted to show the most powerful men in the game that she could be as good as they were. She did and they were after her – her fragile allegiances with other women merely signalled at through her various employee escorts – hardly an allegiance between equals. Jessica's Molly curiously is not a dissimilar character from Maya, in terms of her own system of values and ethics, and her determination to stick to them 'no matter what' makes her Antigone like. Her relationship with her lawyer, a black man played by Idris Elba, offers a refreshing departure from the relentlessly white leading men surrounding the nasty woman in contemporary cinema. Molly is also interesting as a *neo femme fatale* as she inhabits a body and outfits which are usually associated with a *femme fatale*; she is beautiful and sexy, her make-up and outfits emphasise her beauty and her sexuality which she appears to own – except that throughout the whole film there is no suggestion whatever of Molly being a sexual being or even having any relationships with other people outside the poker game or her relationship with her father. It is this representation of this character which has been commented on as unrealistic[4] but one can understand that this nasty woman comes in a straight line from the tradition of virginal characters who put their own determination and desire above anything else.

However fascinating these films are, they do not offer any ways of imagining new allegiances out of the Oedipal cycle. To begin to imagine these we need to look elsewhere.

Intersectionality and fairytales

'Intersectionality' in some guises has been mentioned before in this volume as it connects to the work of Audre Lorde and Sara Ahmed discussed in particular in the chapter on *Gone Girl*. The notion draws from the work of Kimberlé Williams Crenshaw in the late 80s and 90s in which she famously pointed to the ineffectuality of Western (white) feminism and stressed different forms of discrimination converging often in a multi-fronted prejudice against women of colour in particular (Crenshaw 1989: 139). Intersectionality, the notion that subjectivity is constituted by mutually reinforcing vectors of race, gender, class, ability and sexuality, has emerged as the primary theoretical tool designed to combat (feminist) hierarchy, hegemony and other forms of exclusivity and dominance.

The poet and writer Audre Lorde developed the concept further, focusing on the necessity of finding tools of struggle outside 'the master's house'. Many scholars and writers have used it since, challenging 'white' feminism to examine its inherent privilege and re-position the tactics that fight prejudice and inequality. The key point of these two thinkers is that recognising the cumulative effects of discrimination is the first step in combating each individual manifestation. 'Intersectionality' has been critiqued by some scholars (for example Nash 2008: 3) as possibly conflating identity with oppression and thereby being necessarily pessimistic about the effectiveness of local and partial struggles. It is important here to mention even in passing that Lorde's poetic work attempts to enlarge the notion of 'intersectionality'. In Keating's words, 'Lorde extends her experience outwards to include all – regardless of colour, sexuality, gender, age, or class – who do not fit this country's "mythical norm"' (1998: 27). Lorde turns identity politics' project of essential difference into a *coalitional* effort across the systems of domination. This same ethos is pivotal to intersectionality, which by definition questions logics of domination and creates transformative social models (see May 2015: 4). It is in this spirit that I evoke a final few thoughts.

My remarks want to extend intersectionality to include recent work by feminist scholar Donna Haraway urging a step outside determined and deterministic ways of thinking. It is interesting to think about the nomadic ideas by Braidotti and Haraway as lighthouses offering a direction in a sea of hopelessness and rage. This is important especially when transgressing cultural and societal boundaries and limitations and entering spaces of desire. I will be drawing on a cinematic example, using as my case study a recent popular film.

Before I proceed to my final thoughts, I would like to consider my own position here, as reflecting on intersectionality as a non-black scholar. Writing on *Precious* (Lee Daniels, US, 2010), Katariina Kyrölä notes with sensitivity the difficulties involved for white scholars who are interested in discussing the cultural politics of 'race' and ethnicity: 'How we see ourselves (and others) as ethical subjects relates intimately to not only how we feel about things, but to how we feel we *should* feel about things, and to how we express, articulate and intellectually process those feelings' (2017: 258). Highlighting the crucial significance of bell hooks's (2003: 26) work on 'learnt helplessness', Kyrölä cautions against 'a white liberal attitude towards racism which, despite acknowledging racist structures and one's own privilege enabled by them, helps keep whiteness and white (bad) feeling in the center' (2017: 258).

It is beyond the scope of these concluding remarks to begin to debate the right to use different ideas outside one's obvious cultural belonging. Since I have done it throughout this work, without giving it a justification as intellectual freedom, it must mean that – in the same way I have taken issue with the notion of (not) quoting white male thinkers – I take for granted my right to use ideas and theories stemming from a different cultural and intellectual background. Furthermore, I believe that it is important to broaden one's intellectual playground. Clearly one way of beginning to do such work involves reflexive scholarly practice that is grounded in and informed by Black scholarship and its various commentaries on the ontological silences and epistemological failures of unthinkingly white theory, whilst allowing for one's own voice to be heard. In the context of the 'nasty woman' I now turn briefly to a film which to my mind offers some kind of different way of thinking about structural positions in society.

The Shape of Water (2017), directed by Guillermo de Toro – about a romance between a mute cleaner and a male mermaid creature – might not seem to be an obvious contender for a discussion of the nasty woman or even intersectionality. And yet, I would argue, there are many interesting elements to consider here. First, the notion of an alien creature in a *space* dominated by powerful inconsiderate brutal white men who are either military or connected to military could be considered as a metaphor for the organisation of the world as a whole in which the white man still subjugates the Other, be it a woman or a black man. The film produces a clear statement regarding the position of the disadvantaged subject vis-à-vis the system. It is important that the action takes place during the height of the Cold War, a space which serves here as a marker of exclusion (pre-Civil Rights, pre-liberation of homosexuality, pre-disability provisions). Second, the notion of female agency enacted by a disabled woman in an alliance with a black woman offers an interesting way of thinking of it as a positive representation of female friendship in which 'intersectionality' is recognised but where its inevitable and pessimistic outcome is challenged. To take this further, one could venture too that the disabled female character, with apparently limited resources and education, is indeed pushed by the circumstances yet again to become pretty nasty and, and this, crucially, enables her to carry out her final audacious deed *only* in a group effort of an alliance of apparent disadvantaged misfits. This radical gesture against patriarchy aimed to save the ultimate Other becomes also an empowering experience of solidarity which offers glimpses of a different world. The film then, despite its fantastical fairy tale storyworld, offers a proposition of a space in which a substantive change can happen and indeed does. It invites the viewer to enter such a space as an exercise in a different kind of thinking, a moment which Donna Haraway identifies as crucial in the contemporary world. I will return to this point further down.

The narrative of the *The Shape of the Water* centres on a mute cleaning lady Elisa falling in love with a mysterious fishman who is kept in a water tank in a laboratory-cum-military compound for some kind of medical experimentation and finally vivisection. As mentioned, both society at large and the community at the compound are presented to the viewer as traditional, patriarchal, and right wing. Elisa and her gay male friend Giles, who is a disadvantaged unemployed artist (it appears because of his sexuality), live at the margins. Elisa by the virtue of her difference – she is mute and shy – can only do the least prestigious job at the compound and is befriended indeed by a black woman whose own issues are also earmarked by her asymmetrical and problematic relationship with her husband. The latter, we learn, is an unconscious supporter of the white man's patriarchal system, almost a textbook demonstration of someone who, in Audre Lorde's words, is 'using the master's tools',[5] and partakes in the subjugation of a black woman.

It is into this space that the mysterious fishman is brought into. He is humiliated and tortured by the white man in charge, the obnoxious misogynist and caricatured baddie, Strickland. Strickland's conduct, way of thinking and demeanour could be thought of as farcical and overdrawn, except that we all know men of this kind and one of them is the leader of the free world right now. In de Toro's storyworld the water creature's extreme otherness is mediated by its beauty (the athletic body, regular facial features etc) as well as super powers which become obvious in due course. It would have been wonderful if the filmmaker had dared to leave the gender of the mermaid/man as ambivalent (as in *The Untamed* (2016) discussed in Chapter 4) but, unfortunately, the gender is confirmed – as male – which perhaps is slightly disappointing and a nod to the film's Hollywood hallmark.

The water creature is not human but, as Donna Haraway would say, it belongs to the world of this planet, Gaia. It is a most basic observation that physically the water creature is not white – and is positioned purposefully as the exact opposite of Strickland. Its unknowable difference and athletic beauty is considered dangerous and threatening and therefore not worthy of respect by the chief white man in a series of scenes reminiscent of a white man humiliating a black man, for example in films such *12 Years a Slave* (2013) or *Django Unchained* (2012). The scenes of extreme violence towards the fishman are disturbing and rarely mentioned in the reviews but they are important in bringing back the space of the unreasonable and irrational discrimination to the perception of the viewer, consciously or otherwise. In some way therefore, the fantastical tale could be read as a metaphorical love story which maps out a possible space for an interaction which is not just inter-cultural or interracial, although that too, but indeed inter-species. The revenge and violence are not at the core of this film – a way of creating solidarities which erect an unstoppable barrier to the patriarchal on the one hand and a kind of synergy which is outside the clear lines of the world as we know it on the other. It is my hope and hypothesis that the popularity of the film, both at the Oscars but also with the viewing public, may originate from our desire to subvert the endless cycle of violence and retribution.

The characters in *The Shape of Water* are more important than its narrative, which in part is quite predictable and belongs clearly to the genre of a fairy tale with the familiar theme of 'love overcomes all'. However, in the film all the leading characters outside the societal norms are either straightforwardly disadvantaged (disabled, female, black or gay), and/ or have complicated relationships with the external world. They succeed against all the odds at that particular moment in time when the viewer knows that they would have been the exact victims of an intersectional prejudice whereas in the film they succeed by bonding and solidarity – I suggest that there is a way of thinking about this as a radical gesture and a manifesto not miles away from Donna Haraway's 'string figuring' which demands a different ways of thinking of the world, including re-positioning of its possible spaces and structures.

In her new book *Staying with the Trouble* (2016), Haraway urges a way of thinking about the world which moves away from hitherto accepted traditions, including the reduction of differences to binary oppositions. This re-thinking, however idealistic it might be, offers a chance for the world to re-define itself. She calls such a thinking Tentacular Thinking or string figuring (SF). One could argue that this position is against any configurations, which could be considered limiting or pessimistic, including arguably 'intersectionality'. Haraway urges instead an attempt to think outside the rigid boundaries of binaries. She suggests an effort is made to find 'in-between' spaces in which new allegiances might be possible and therefore the world will have to change. The first step is to think out of the position of Antropocene, that is out of the human position.

Haraway insists on the importance of stories that create spaces for different thinking: 'It matters what thoughts think thoughts. It matters what knowledges know knowledges. It matters what relations relate relations. It matters what worlds world worlds. It matters what stories tell stories' (2016: 35). *The Shape of Water* tells a story which allows for a space of the string figuring, meaning alternative ways of thinking about the world to take place. Haraway urges us to be encouraged to think of the non-human life as a life from which one can learn. In the film, the important link between Eliza and the creature is their shared lack, the inability to speak, but also their presumed courage in the face of ultimate adversity.

Haraway insists on re-configuring the thoughts we allow ourselves to think, for example regarding the limits of our relationships. She quotes Isabelle Stengers:

> More precisely, com-menting, if it means thinking-with, that is becoming-with, is in itself a way of relaying. . . . But knowing that what you take has been held out entails a particular thinking 'between.' It does not demand fidelity, still less fealty, rather a particular kind of loyalty, the answer to the trust of the held out hand. Even if this trust is not in 'you' but in 'creative uncertainty.'
>
> (Stengers, in Haraway 2016: 34)

Haraway talks about 'nonarrogant collaboration' – across cultures, races and species (2016: 56). It is this kind of 'nonarrogant collaboration' which *The Shape of Water* speaks to, transcending to my mind 'intersectionality' within its fantastical world on the one hand, and the cruelty meted out to the underprivileged on the other.

Haraway insists: We are all with those in the muddle. We are all lichens; so we can be scraped off the rocks by the Furies, who still erupt to avenge crimes against the earth. Alternatively, we can join 'in the metabolic transformations between and among rocks and critters for living and dying well' (2016: 56). In *The Shape of Water* Eliza ends up indeed in a

Figure 5.1 The mysterious 'fishman' (Doug Jones) and Eliza (Sally Hawkins) in *The Shape of Water*

(Guillermo del Toro 2017)

possible metabolic transformation, however utopian it might be, which offers an alternative happy ending in a story that was heading for a more realistic disaster.

Its fantastical and Hollywood solutions notwithstanding, the film opens a new space for imagining of transformations for a viewer who may have never heard of intersectionality or Donna Haraway. In the storyworld of *The Shape of Water* it is telling that Elisa has to become pretty nasty to carry out her deed of rescuing the water creature from the evil lab – it still appears a necessary stage in whatever imaginings might ensue.

This short volume focused on a few chosen cinematic texts in English language. They have either been directed by women or based on the works generated or written by women. For the purpose of this work, I have bracketed important films featuring powerful women in other parts of the world but it is clear that the nasty woman has making changes across the globe, both in cinema and in culture. For example, the French filmmaker Catherine Breillat has long been shifting perspectives and para-digms by making challenging films about female (and male) bodies. The Polish filmmaker Malgorzata Szumowska has made films questioning female sexuality on the one hand and notions of honesty on the other, for example. Indian female filmmakers are rising to make their voices heard with quite extraordinary works such as *Parched* (2016) written and directed by Leena Yadav or *Lipstick under the Burka* directed by Alankrita Shrivastava. And with her film *Playing Warriors* (2011) Rumbi Katedza in Zimbabwe named the issues surrounding patriarchy giving her fictional characters based on real women courage not to be 'nice' at all times.

The road is hard if rewarding. It might be that soon the nasty woman will be ready to transform herself into another creation – as long as it does not involve being subjugated and mistreated by the representatives of patriarchy. She knows that it is important to imagine another world, in which binaries are got rid of – finally. The project is perhaps utopian and yet it is important to insist on it as a creative way forward.

For the moment, the nastiness of a woman remains a necessary pos-sibility even though we do know that what we want in culture and in life is a celebration of the 'creative uncertainty' and thinking with 'those who are not like us'.

Notes

1 www.capitalfm.co.ke/news/2018/06/harvey-weinstein-set-plead-innocent-ny/ (accessed 4 June 2018).
   A further development discussed here with the case going to court:

https://edition.cnn.com/2018/06/05/us/harvey-weinstein-arraignment/index. html (accessed 5 June 2018).

www.newyorker.com/news/news-desk/behind-the-scenes-of-harvey-weinsteins-impending-arrest (accessed 5 June 2018).

2 www.indy100.com/article/harvey-weinstein-arrest-sexual-assault-women-detective-metoo-hollywood-8370316 (accessed 5 June 2018).

3 www.independent.co.uk/voices/three-billboards-outside-ebbing-missouri-oscar-nominations-racism-frances-mcdormand-a8174431.html (accessed 5 June).

4 In this review the point of only the women being players is made too: www. theguardian.com/film/2017/dec/28/mollys-game-review-jessica-chastain-aaron-sorkin (accessed 5 June 2018).

5 In the poem 'Between Ourselves', Lorde famously accused the black man of committing the first betrayal of a black woman.

Bibliography

Crenshaw, K. (1989) *Demarginalizing the intersection of race and sex: A black feminist critique of antidiscrimination doctrine, feminist theory, and antiracist politics*. Chicago: University of Chicago Legal Forum.

Haraway, D.J. (2016) *Staying with the trouble: Making kin in the Chthulucene*. Durham: Duke University Press.

hooks, b. (2003) *Teaching community: A pedagogy of hope*. London: Routledge.

Keating, A. (1998) '(De)centering the margins? Identity politics and tactical (re)naming', in Stanley, S.K. (ed.), *Other sisterhoods: Literary theory and U.S. women of color*. Urbana: University of Illinois Press, pp. 23–43.

Kyrölä, K. (2017) 'Feeling bad and *Precious* (2009): Black suffering, white guilt, and intercorporeal subjectivity', *Subjectivity* 10, pp. 258–275.

Lorde, A. (1982) *Zami: A new spelling of my name*. Freedom: The Crossing Press.

Lorde, A. (1995 [1978]) *The black unicorn: Poems*. New York: W. W. Norton.

Lorde, A. (2007 [1984]) *Sister outsider*. Berkeley: Crossing Press.

May, V.M. (2015) *Pursuing intersectionality, unsettling dominant imaginaries*. New York: Routledge.

Nash, J.C. (2008) 'Re-thinking intersectionality', *Feminist Review* 89, pp. 1–15.

Index

Note: Page numbers in italic indicate a figure on the corresponding page.

abuse 6–7, 33, 55–56, 99, 105, 107
action 1, 16
agency 3, 8–9, 14–15, 19, 107–108, 111;
    the feminist killjoy and 44, 46, 48–49,
    55, 62; *Red Road* and 86–88, 94;
    Stories We Tell and 70, 77, 81; *Zero
    Dark Thirty* and 25, 27, 29, 33, 35
Ahmed, Sara 3, 109; and the feminist
    killjoy 44, 45–46, 56, 58, 60–62, 63n5
Akerman, Chantal 5, 59; *see also
    Jeanne Dielman*
allegiance 4, 20, 59–60, 108–109, 113
anger 6–7, *43*, 48–49, 56–58, 107, 110;
    and *Red Road* 86, 102; and *Stories
    We Tell* 75
Antigone 2, 9, 26–30, 41n7, 58; and
    Stories We Tell 65, 75–76, 80; and
    Zero Dark Thirty 13–16, 19–20,
    22n16, 22n17, 32–40
Antonioni, Michelangelo 89
Arnold, Andrea 63, 85–87, 93–96, 101,
    102n1; *see also Red Road*
Atë 9, 30, 34–37, 40, 41n5
Athena 6–7, 13, 18
Austen, Jane 9
autism 27–28, 34

Bakhtin, Mikhail 47
Balázs, Béla 39, 81
Barker, Jennifer 40, 102
beauty 13–14, 16, 54, 56, 109, 112; and
    Stories We Tell 76; and *Zero Dark
    Thirty* 28–29, 36–40

Bergstrom, Janet 11
Bigelow, Kathryn 25–28, 33–34, 36,
    38; *see also Zero Dark Thirty*
binaries 4, 20, 21n5, 106, 113, 115; and
    the feminist killjoy 44, *43*, 59; and
    Stories We Tell 82, 89, 96–97
Bizet, George 9
Blow Up 89
Blue Velvet 17, 44–46, 52, 55–57,
    59–60, 89
body, the 17; and *Red Road* 86, 88, 92,
    95, 101; and *Stories We Tell* 70; and
    Zero Dark Thirty 32–33, 40
Bolton, Lucy 11
Braidotti, Rosi 4, 21n5, 106, 110;
    see also Nomadic Theory
Breuer, Josef 18–19
Bronte, Emily 9
Brown, William 27–28, 33–34, 40, 41n7
Burgoyne, Robert 32–33, 38–40
Butler, Judith 6, 14–15, 22n16, 29,
    41n3, 60

Cake 87–88, 90, 95
Carmen 9
Carruthers, Susan L. 38, 40
castration 18, 54–55, 96
Cixous, Hélène 6, 44, 63n1
class 36, 45, 60–61, 108–110
Clinton, Hillary 2–3, 11, 20n4
Collins, K. Austin 25–27
Conversation, The 89–90
cool girl 5–6, 12–13, 48–49, 55, 58–59

Coppola, Frances Ford 89
courtesans 1, 9
Cowie, Elizabeth 11, 13
Crenshaw, Kimberlé Williams 109

Dangerembga, Tsitsi 21n6
death 9, 14, 22n17, *43*, 58, 107; death
    drive 19, 90, 99–100; and *Red Road*
    87; and *Stories We Tell* 76–77; and
    Zero Dark Thirty 29, 39
de Beauvoir, Simone 45, 57
deception 17, 66, 73, 77, 82, 85
defence 25, 67, 82
de Lauretis, Teresa 6
Dern, Laura 6, 53, 59
desire 8, 15–16, 19, 21n13, 109–110,
    113; ethics of 28–32; and the killjoy
    43–46, *43*, 57–60; and misogyny 49,
    53–57; and *Red Road* 86–87, 89–92,
    94–96, 98–102; and *Stories We Tell*
    65, 67–69, 76, 79–81; and *Zero Dark
    Thirty* 27, 34, 36–38, 40, 41n2
documentary 6, 17, 85, 108; ethical
    gesture in 37, 78–81; and the killjoy
    63; and *Stories We Tell* 68–69,
    71–72, 76–77, 82
Dumas, Alexandre 9

ecriture feminine 44, 63n1
Elizabeth I 15
embodiment *43*, 61, 71–72, 81, 97,
    101, 108
ethics 4, 13–15, *43*, 108, 110;
    reviewing and 78–81; and *Stories
    We Tell* 66, 68–70, 72–73, 75–77,
    82; and *Zero Dark Thirty* 28–32, 34,
    36–40

fairytales 2–3, 7, 13, 21n6: and
    intersectionality 109–115
family 14, 17, 107; and *Red Road*
    87–88, 90, 96; and *Stories We Tell*
    65–70, 73–77, 80, 82; and *Zero Dark
    Thirty* 29; *see also* kinship
fantasy 5, 9, 14–16, 101; and the killjoy
    44–46, *43*, 48, 52–53, 55–56, 59–60;
    and *Red Road* 88; and *Stories We
    Tell* 77
Farrimond, Katherine 17
fear 7, 18, *43*

female subjectivity 10–14, 17
feminine, the 11, 19, 44, 53, 56, 62;
    Antigone and 32, 36; *see also
    jouissance*
feminism 2–3, 5–6, 8, 10–14, 16–18,
    20, 22n16; and the killjoy 43–46, *43*,
    55–62; and *Zero Dark Thirty* 26, 29
femininity *see* feminine, the
femme fatale 1–2, 8, 12, 15–17; and
    the killjoy 45–46, 55, 60–61; and
    Red Road 85–86, 99, 102; and *Zero
    Dark Thirty* 40; *see also* neo *femme
    fatale*
filmmaking 11, 68, 75, 77, 82; and
    Stories We Tell 70–73
Fincher, David 12, 50, 52; *see also
    Gone Girl*
Flynn, Gillian 5, 12, 46, 48–52, 58–59;
    see also Gone Girl
Foucault, Michel 68, 79–81, 103n3;
    and reviewing the self 77–78
Fox, Jennifer 6
Freudianism 6, 54, 70, 81
Freud, Sigmund 8, 18–19, 108; and the
    ethical act 30; and the killjoy 52–53,
    55, 63; and *Red Road* 94, 99–100;
    and *Stories We Tell* 67, 69, 75;
    see also Freudianism
Fuss, Diana 6

gaze 13–14, 18, 33–35, 38, 69, 86
gender 5–6, 11, 21n5, 22n16, 109–110,
    112; gender identity 2, 21n5; and the
    killjoy 43–44, 48, 53, 58, 60, 63n1;
    and *Red Road* 96, 98; and *Stories We
    Tell* 82; and *Zero Dark Thirty* 25, 29,
    37, 39–40, 41n3
Gentileschi, Artemisia 7–8
Girl on the Train, The 16, 19, 43–46,
    60–63, 107; female subjectivity and
    11–12, 14; the killjoy and 57–59;
    misogyny and 46–50, 56
Goethe, Johann Wolfgang von 6, 29
Gone Girl 43–46, *51*, 59–63, 107, 109;
    and female subjectivity 10–14; the
    killjoy and 57–59; misogyny and
    46–50, *51*, 52, 56–57; and the nasty
    woman 3, 5; and the neo *femme
    fatale* 16–17, 19, 86, 102
Grant, Catherine 11

Haraway, Donna 4, 59, 106, 110–115
Hawkins, Paula 12, 46, 48; *see also*
    Girl on the Train
heteronormativity 9, 57, 97, 103n3
Hitchcock, Alfred 89
Holofernes *see* Judith
homosexuality 16, 93, 98, 111, 113;
    see also queer theory
Honig, Bonnie 14, 29, 38
Horeck, Tanya 11
horror 1, 18; and the killjoy 46, 52, 54;
    and *Red Road* 87, 97; and *Stories We
    Tell* 76; and *Zero Dark Thirty* 29–30,
    32, 34, 37–40
housewife 5, 59
hysteria 8, 15, 18–19, 52

ideas 14, 108, 110; and the killjoy
    43–44, *43*, 57, 60; and *Red Road* 97,
    102; and *Stories We Tell* 78; and *Zero
    Dark Thirty* 29
identity 4, 56, 66, 82, 100, 109–110
Imaginary, the 13, 33, 69
insanity 8, 15, 19
intersectionality 60, 109–115
Irigaray, Luce 14, 22n16, 62
I, Tonya 107–108

Jeanne Dielman 5, *5*, 45, 59
Joan of Arc 15
Johnston, C. 11
Johnston, Elizabeth 21n11
jouissance 86, 88, 95, 97, 99–101, 102n2
Judith 1, 8

Khanna, Ranjana 94–95
Kieslowski, Krzysztof 87, 89, 100–101
killjoy 3, 5, 45–46, 57–59, 63
kinship 22n16, 65
Klein, Melanie 71, 81

Lacanianism 6, 48, 63n1; and *Red Road*
    86, 88, 97; and *Stories We Tell* 65,
    81–82; and *Zero Dark Thirty* 28–29,
    36, 41n7
Lacan, Jacques 8, 13–16; and the
    killjoy 58, 60; and *Red Road* 89,
    95, 100–101, 102n2, 103n3; and
    Stories We Tell 69–70, 72, 75–76,
    79–80; and *Zero Dark Thirty* 27,

30–34, 37–38, 40, 41n2, 41n3, 41n4;
    see also Lacanianism
Levinas, Emmanuel 27, 69, 77–79
Lewinsky, Monika 21n9
Lorde, Audre 46, 62, 87, 107,
    109–110, 112
love 8–9, 13, 18–19, *43*, 48, 52, 111–113;
    and *Red Road* 87, 95–97, 99–101;
    and *Stories We Tell* 65, 67, 69, 81; and
    Zero Dark Thirty 30–32, 38
Lynch, David 44–46, 52, 54, 56;
    see also Blue Velvet

Marks, Laura 71, 102
Marso, Lori 45, 57
Marxism 102–103n3
masculine, the 1, 44, 53, 56, 60; *Red
    Road* and 88, 106–107; *Zero Dark
    Thirty* and 29, 36
masculinity *see* masculine, the
Mayer, Sophie 11
McGowan, Rose 7, 106
Medusa 6–10
melancholia 19–20, 90, 94–95
metaphor 6, 19, 107, 112; and the
    killjoy 43–44, *43*, 45–46, 49–50, 56,
    58–59; and *Red Road* 94–95; and
    Zero Dark Thirty 27, 41n7
#MeToo 1–6
Metropolitan Museum of Art 1, 6
misogyny 2, *43*, 45–47, 49, 52, 112
Molly's Game 107–108
monstrosity 7, 14–16, 18, 100, 105;
    Zero Dark Thirty and 27, 35, 37
mourning 20, 39, 69, 94
Mulvey, Laura 13, 53–56

nastiness 4–5, 8–9, 12, 15, 17, 19–20,
    115; and the killjoy 46; and *Stories
    We Tell* 67, 82
nasty woman 1–6, 105–109; Antigone
    as 14–15; mad nasty women 6–10;
    neo *femme fatale* versus 16–20;
    see also nastiness
Negri, Pola 9
neo *femme fatale* 10, 14–16, 22n17, 57,
    65, 109; versus the nasty woman 16–20
niceness 2–3, 7, 14, 47, 58, 115
nomadic theory 4, *43*, 59–63, 110
Nomadic Theory 4

obsolescence *see* obsolete technology
obsolete technology 68, 73–77, 81
Osterwell, Ara 11

patriarchy 2–3, 5–9, 11–13, 15–17,
    19–20, 22n16, 22n17; and the
    killjoy 43, 47, 49, 55–58, 60–62,
    63n1; nomadic remarks on 106–108,
    111–112, 115; and *Red Road* 88; and
    Stories We Tell 65, 67–68, 70, 74–75,
    82; and *Zero Dark Thirty* 27, 35, 40
performance 18, 33, 70–73, 108
performativity 21n5, 41n3, 70–73, 85
Plato 99–101
political, the 2, 11–12, 25, 56, 67,
    92–96, 103n3
Polley, Sarah 17, 63, 66–71, 73–77,
    79–80, 82, 107; *see also Stories
    We Tell*
pornography 92–93
post-human, the 4, 34, 40, *43*, 89
Puccini, Giacomo 9
psychoanalysis 8, 17–18; and the
    killjoy *43*, 52–53, 56, 60; and *Red
    Road* 86, 94, 99; and *Stories We Tell*
    67–68, 70, 72, 76, 81; and *Zero Dark
    Thirty* 31, 38, 40

queer theory 21n5, 102–103n3
Quinlivan, Davina 11, 70–71, 77, 81, 102

race 39, *43*, 61, 109–110
racism *43*, 107, 110
Radcliffe, Ann 9
rage *see* anger
rape 6–7, 21n11, 41n7, 91, 95, 105
Real, the 13, 33, 40, 86, 95
Red Road 10–11, 14–16, 19–20, 63,
    85–92, *91*, 107; and sex 92–96; and
    tentacular thinking 96–102
reparation 68, 70–73, 77, 81–82
reviewing 77–82
Riefenstahl, Leni 26
Rose, Jacqueline 45–47, 49–50, 63n2

Sandberg, Cheryl 12
scholarship 17, *43*, 63n1, 110; and
    Stories We Tell 67, 70, 72, 77
Scott, Walter 9
self-care 68, 79–80

self-reflection 68, 79–80
sex 2, 47–48, 52–53; as political
    gesture 92–96; and *Red Road* 87,
    90–94, *91*, 96–101; and *Stories We
    Tell* 69, 75; and *Zero Dark Thirty* 30,
    38–39; *see also* sexuality
sexual assault *see* sexual violence
sexuality 107, 109–110, 112, 115;
    Antigone and 15; female subjectivity
    and 12; and the killjoy 44, 62; the
    nasty woman and 3, 8–9; and the neo
    femme fatale 16, 20; and *Red Road*
    85, 103n3; and *Stories We Tell* 65
sexual privilege 13
sexual violence 6–10, 14–15;
    see also rape
Seyrig, Delphine 5
Shakespeare, William 8–9
Shape of Water, The 111, 113–115, *114*
Short Film About Love, A 89, 101
Showalter, Elaine 8
Silverman, Kaja 10
sinthome 73–76, 82
Sobchack, Vivian 71, 81, 102
Soler, Colette 18, 67
solidarity 2, 13, 57, 61–62, 92, 113
Sophocles 14, 16, 28–29, 32, 34
Stories We Tell 65–69, *66*, 81–82, 107;
    and childhood trauma 69–70; and
    female subjectivity 10–11, 14; and
    Foucault 77–78; and the neo *femme
    fatale* 17, 19; obsolete technology
    in 73–75; and reparation 70–73; and
    reviewing 78–81; and sublimation
    75–77
storyworld 3, 10, 12, 20, 108, 111–112,
    115; and *Red Road* 86, 94
subjectivity 46, 60, 72, 102, 109;
    see also female subjectivity
sublimation 8, 38, 67, 73–77, 89
Symbolic, the 13, 19, 33, 63n1, 69
Symposium 99–100

Tale, The 6
Taylor, Tate 12, 50; *see also Girl on the
    Train, The*
technology *43*; and *Red Road* 85–86,
    88–89; and *Stories We Tell* 67–68,
    79, 81–82; *see also* obsolete
    technology

tentacular thinking 96–102, 113
Three Billboards Outside Ebbing, Missouri 107
Three Colours Blue 87, 90, 95
time 4, *43*, 56, 91
transference 6, 67–69
trauma 3, 8, 20, 53, 106; and *Red Road* 86, 88–89; and *Stories We Tell* 66–70, 73–74, 76, 82; and *Zero Dark Thirty* 27, 29–30, 32–33, 38
Tree of Life, The 45
Trump, Donald 2–3, 11

Untamed, The 97–101, 112

Verdi, Giuseppe 9
virginal, the 15, 109
violence 19, 44–46, *43*, 106–107, 112–113; and lost desire 57, 59; and misogyny 49–52, 55–57; and *Red Road* 95; and *Stories We Tell* 74; and *Zero Dark Thirty* 27–28, 30, 36, 39–40
voice 8, 10–14, 19, 47, 51, 60–61

Walpole, Horace 8–9
Weinstein, Harvey 3–4, 7, 54, 105–106
Wilson, Emma 11, 86, 102
Wilson, Erin Cressida 12
Winnicott, Donald 69
witch 3, 21n6
Wolf, Naomi 26

Zero Dark Thirty 25–28, *35*, 40, 106, 108; and Antigone 32–34; and Atë 34–37; beauty versus horror in 37–40; and the ethics of desire 28–32; and female subjectivity 11, 14; and the neo *femme fatale* 16, 19–20
Žižek, Slavoj 15, 25, 27–28, 36–37, *36*, 41n7

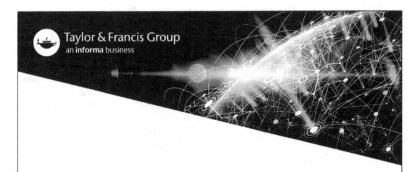

Printed in the United States
by Baker & Taylor Publisher Services